SNAKES OF THE WORLD

SNAKES OF THE WORLD

PETER BRAZAITIS AND MYRNA E. WATANABE

CRESCENT BOOKS
New York/Avenel, New Jersey

A FRIEDMAN GROUP BOOK

This 1992 edition published by Crescent Books, distributed by
Outlet Book Company, Inc., a Random House Company,
34 Englehard Avenue, Avenel, New Jersey 07001.

ISBN 0-517-02326-1

SNAKES OF THE WORLD
was prepared and produced by
Michael Friedman Publishing Group, Inc.
15 West 26th Street
New York, New York 10010

Editors: Sharyn Rosart and Kelly Matthews
Art Direction: Devorah Levinrad
Designer: Maura Fadden Rosenthal
Photography Editor: Christopher C. Bain
Photo Research: Grace How

Typeset by Trufont Typographers
Color separations by Rainbow Graphic Arts Co.
Printed and bound in Hong Kong by Leefung-Asco Printers Ltd.

8   7   6   5   4   3   2   1

To Peter, a herpetologist in the making, with love

ACKNOWLEDGMENTS

This book was made possible with the help of many people. We thank our good friend Dr. Warren Wetzel of Albert Einstein College of Medicine for writing much of the information on snakebite treatment, Steve Johnson of the New York Zoological Society's library who answered numerous calls and e-mail messages that he could have ignored; and our friend and colleague Itzchak Gilboa of City University of New York who was always available for midnight consultations. Thanks also are due to Mark Wise and Greg Lepera of the St. Augustine Alligator Farm; Robin Lepore of the Office of the Solicitor General, U.S. Fish and Wildlife Service, Boston; Tom Mason of the Reptile Breeding Foundation, Picton, Ontario, Canada; and Richard Luxmoore, World Conservation Monitoring Centre, Cambridge, U.K. We especially want to thank our editors at the Michael Friedman Publishing Group, who have done a terrific job: Sharyn Rosart and Kelly Matthews. We also thank Maura Fadden Rosenthal, Chris Bain, and Devorah Levinrad at Friedman for their excellent work in graphic design and photograph selection and placement.

Peter gives special thanks to Richard Lattis and the New York Zoological Society for their many years of support and for helping to create an atmosphere of professionalism in which to work.

Most of all, we thank Dr. Herndon G. Dowling, the ultimate snake man, who taught us everything we know.

Peter Brazaitis
Myrna E. Watanabe
November 25, 1991

CONTENTS

INTRODUCTION

Sinister and evil by reputation and superstition, feared, reviled, and thought of as vermin—these are common attitudes people hold toward snakes. Such feelings are often deeply rooted in how snakes are depicted to children by parents, in religious beliefs, in superstitions, and in stories often told of unexpected and, perhaps, terrifying encounters with snakes.

Yet if we step back for a moment and look at the snake as a living creature like any other that shares this Earth with us, we find one of the most amazing, diverse, little-known, and interesting of animals, useful and perhaps even necessary to humanity in a wide variety of ways. We find a creature that even is worshiped by certain peoples. Snakes exist in nearly every warm or temperate part of the world. While some snakes may live around or even in our homes, with or without our consent, others are at home in the torrid deserts, tropical rain forests, and jungles. Still other snakes frequent the open seas, live high in trees, and even fly. Each form has adapted in many ways to a highly specialized style of existence.

Some snakes are venomous and pose a danger to humans. These species are few in number, and the potential threat they pose is often exaggerated, not to mention universally applied to all snakes by the misinformed. Yet in recent years, scientists have discovered that even the venomous species are highly useful creatures, with venoms so complex and efficient in their design and

Venom glands take up a lot of space, requiring a large head size.

© David T. Roberts

function that purified components from them can be used to study human disease and the complex neurological functions of our bodies.

An interest in snakes, which as a professional study is part of the science of herpetology, is not reserved for a few strange people of questionable wisdom. Many a distraught parent has found that while they were retreating from nightmarish stories about snakes, their children were discovering the fascination of a living animal that harbored no dangerous diseases, did not elicit the discomfort of allergies, and frequently provided a service in controlling harmful rodent populations. This book is meant to excite and bolster that interest in the fascinating world of these unique creatures. Their preservation as part of our wildlife heritage should be no less than what we afford any other creature.

The common garter snake, *Thamnophis sirtalis*, is nonvenomous and found throughout North America. There are twelve subspecies.

ORIGINS AND EVOLUTION

*S*nakes existed on Earth for more than 100 million years before humans' earliest primate ancestors evolved. This means that snakes, no matter how revolting or captivating we may find them, have an earlier claim on our planet. But where did snakes come from? The fossil record indicates that snakes must have evolved from some other reptilian group during or before the early Cretaceous period, some 140 million years ago.

One hundred forty million years is actually a short time in the history of reptiles. Reptiles had already been on earth for more than 150 million years by the time snakes evolved. Thus in the reptilian scheme of evolution, snakes are relative newcomers. The earliest reptiles evolved during the Pennsylvanian epoch of the Carboniferous period during the late Paleozoic era, approximately 300 million years ago. The earliest reptiles, the captorhinomorphs, were very different from present-day snakes. They had heavily boned skulls with no openings, save for the eye sockets, and they were quadrupedal, having four sprawled legs. During the late Paleozoic and into the Mesozoic eras, a period of more than 100 million years, the many different groups of reptiles developed: turtles; crocodilian ancestors and dinosaurs; rhychocephalians, which are represented today by two species of tuatara living on islands off the New Zealand coast; lizards; and then snakes. Taxonomists, the scientists who study the classification of organisms, and vertebrate paleontologists, who study the history and evolution of vertebrates (backboned creatures), do not know from which reptilian group snakes evolved. Some scientists theorize that snakes evolved from lizards, and cite similarities between living snakes and either the living earless monitor lizard, *Lanthanotus borneensis*, a rare lizard present in only a few localities in Borneo, or some of the geckolike lizards. Others believe that lizards and snakes evolved independently of each other, possibly from a

common ancestor. The Amphisbaenia or ringed lizards, which are not really lizards at all but soft-bodied burrowing creatures, some lacking limbs, may possibly be closely related to snakes.

Taxonomists rely upon certain characteristics of the vertebrae, or backbones, to determine relationships among fossil snakes. Because many snakes are small and delicate, snake fossils may be lacking many of the vertebrae, which may have been scattered throughout many sites, or they may have been crushed. The resulting lack of evidence causes difficulties for taxonomists in determining the evolution of snakes. This is further compounded by the relative scarcity of snake fossils.

Although fossil snakes have been found worldwide, the oldest fossils, dating from the early Cretaceous period, perhaps about 140 million years old, were found in northern Africa. This location, of course, may have no meaning as far as establishing the site of the initial evolution of snake species and their subsequent distribution, as it is possible that older snake fossils are yet to be uncovered or cannot be clearly identified as bones of snakes

The Cape spade-snouted worm lizard, *Monopeltis capensis*, is similar in structure to animals that may be the forebears of modern snakes. As in snakes, one lung is greatly reduced. Earliest amphisbaenian fossils are more than 65 million years old.

© John Visser

due to their poor condition. Fossils from later in the Cretaceous period, about 60 million years after the continents separated, have been found worldwide; meaning that even throughout their early existence, snakes were found on all the continents. That snakes were found worldwide by this time indicates that species might have migrated great distances. The north Atlantic Ocean, however, did not completely separate until the lower Eocene epoch, about 55 million years ago, so Eurasia and North America remained linked. The Bering land bridge, linking present-day Alaska with Siberia, which was present through recent times, would have allowed migration of groups from Asia to North America and vice versa.

The puzzle, then, is which group of living snakes is the oldest and does its distribution give a clue to snake evolution? To understand the living snakes, it is important to first understand the taxonomy, or classification, of snakes. If the reader will excuse the pun, this presents a veritable viper's nest, as no two taxonomists agree on a classification scheme.

Fossil snake skeleton.

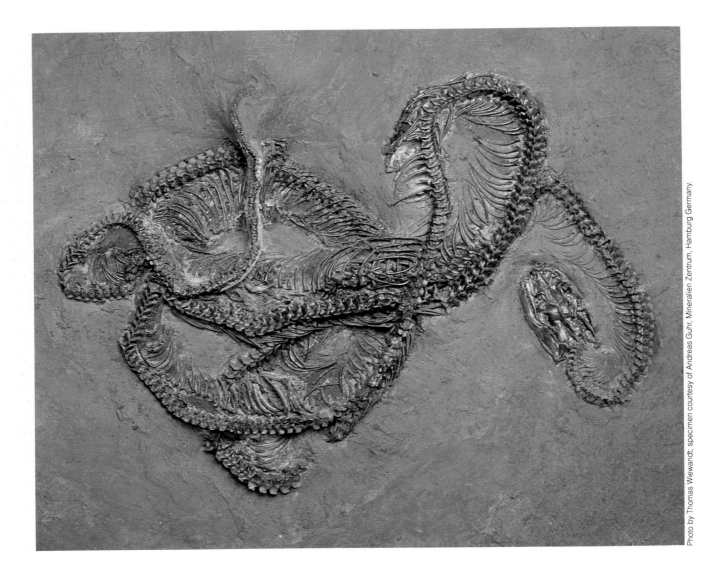

Photo by Thomas Wiewandt; specimen courtesy of Andreas Guhr, Mineralien Zentrum, Hamburg Germany.

CONTINENTAL DRIFT

*T*he theory of continental drift and plate tectonics describes how the seven continents we know today were formed. Two hundred fifty million years ago or more, the Earth's landmasses were concentrated on one side of the globe: today's separate northern continents were linked together, forming one large landmass known as Laurasia, and the southern continents were also linked, forming a huge continent called Gondwanaland. These two landmasses crashed into each other, forming one united mass, which we call Pangaea. Pangaea was intact through the Permian and Triassic periods, between 195 and 250 or more millions of years ago. As reptiles evolved during the Carboniferous period, about 340 to 350 million years ago, fossils of early reptiles may be found throughout the world. During the Jurassic period, 130 to 195 million years ago, Laurasia and Gondwana separated from each other. This separation occurred at about the same time that the earliest snakes are thought to have evolved. Eurasia still maintained a link to Africa and was never far enough away to prevent migration of species between the continents, but for a species evolving in Europe to reach South America, which was still closely attached to Africa, it first would have had to migrate from Eurasia into Africa. By

Between 195 and 250 million years ago, the continents as we know them today were united, forming one landmass called Pangaea (top). About 180 million years ago, the landmass began to separate (center). The continents were very nearly in their current positions about 110 million years ago (bottom).

about 110 million years ago, during the Cretaceous period, the continents were well separated, but South America and Africa probably still maintained some sort of land bridge until 35 or 40 million years ago. South America was also linked to Antarctica, which was attached to Australia. The Indian subcontinent had pulled away from Antarctica and eastern Africa and was well on its journey to Asia. When India crashed into Asia, the shock lifted the earth at the point of collision and created the Himalaya Mountains. Northern North America still remained attached to Eurasia and the northwestern edge of North America began reaching toward the northeastern edge of Asia, eventually creating the Bering land bridge, which allowed vast migrations of animal species from Asia to North America and vice versa. During the Cretaceous period, a temporary land route existed between North and South America, allowing migration of organisms, but the Panamanian land bridge creating Central America did not exist until the Pliocene epoch, 2.5 to 7 million years ago. So, during the early years of snake evolution, the animals living on the South American, North American, and Eurasian landmasses could readily move from one future continent to the next.

Classification attempts to determine the relationships of living things to each other and to their evolutionary history. The classification scheme of animals assigns each animal into subdivisions that are further subdivided until the animal is placed in a grouping of organisms that all appear to be closely related.

The largest grouping, or kingdom, classifies an organism as either an animal, a green plant, a fungus, a protist (a single-celled organism, such as an amoeba, with certain distinct structural

The rhinoceros viper, *Bitis nasi-cornis*, a forest-dwelling viperine of Central Africa. These venomous snakes are relatively recent in origin.

A blind worm snake, *Typhlops schinzi*. Some scientists believe early snakes burrowed and had reduced eyesight, similar to the modern worm snakes.

features), a bacterium, or a virus. A snake would belong to the kingdom Animalia. During embryonic development, the snake has a dorsal structure called the notochord, therefore it is classified in the phylum Chordata, and because it has vertebrae, or a backbone, it is placed in the subphylum Vertebrata, or vertebrates. The snake, having scales and either giving birth to live young or producing leathery-shelled amniote eggs, is a reptile and is further classified into the class Reptilia, which includes all reptiles, both living and extinct. The living reptiles are further subdivided into four orders: turtles, the tuatara, the squamates (including lizards and snakes), and the crocodilians. The snake would be classified in the Squamata, in the suborder Serpentes, the snakes, because it has scales, no eyelids, no limbs, and no external ears.

Living snakes are divided into two infraorders: the relatively primitive Scolecophidia and the rest of the snakes, the Alethinophidia. If we wished to classify a specific snake, such as the boa constrictor, *Boa constrictor*, we would find that it belongs in the superfamily Booidea, family Boidae, and subfamily Boinae. Its generic and specific names, *Boa constrictor*, are Latin names that indicate to scientists all over the world exactly which snake it is. It is, in fact, the only member of the genus *Boa*. Therefore, if we write in this book about *Boa constrictor*, there will be no doubt in the reader's mind as to what snake we mean. But if we were to write about the *macaurel*, a common name used for boas in South America, you would not be able to tell if we were writing about *Boa constrictor* or the garden boa, *Corallus enydris*. Thus, Latin names allow you to identify a species, differentiate between that species and any other species, and give you an idea of the relatedness of the species to other animals. The more closely related two organisms appear to be, the more likely that taxonomists will place them, at the very least, in the same family, if not in the same subfamily or same genus. The classification system is a man-made, and therefore artificial, system. It is not, however, haphazard. There are certain rules that must be followed in order to classify an organism in its most appropriate genus. Structural or developmental characteristics must be shared among closely related organisms.

The earliest fossils that belong to a group of living snakes are classified as possibly members of the family Boidae, the living family of which comprise the boas. These fossils date from between 65 and 80 million years ago. There is some debate among paleontologists and taxonomists as to whether these early animals were really boids, but certainly by about 60 million years ago, boids were present. Boid fossils have been found in Europe, North and South America, and Asia, but the earliest fossils are from continents that made up Gondwana, the landmass thought to have contained Africa, South America, Australia, and Antarctica. It is thought that boids evolved in Gondwana and, during the late Cretaceous, about 65 million years ago, were able to enter North America from South America via a temporary land bridge between the two continents. From North America, boids were able to travel into Europe and Asia, leading to a worldwide distribution. A member of the family Aniliidae, which includes *Anilius*, a burrowing snake from South America, has also been identified from North American strata that are slightly over 60 million years old. Again, it is hypothesized that aniliids also evolved on Gondwana and used the temporary land bridge to move between South America and North America, and then on to Europe and Asia. Both modern boids and aniliids show similar structural features: a rudimentary pelvis and spurs that are remnants of hind limbs.

The next oldest group of snakes is the infraorder Scolecophidia, a group that includes the families Anomalepidae,

The South American boa constrictor, *Boa constrictor*, a member of one of the oldest groups of snakes.

Typhlopidae, and Leptotyphlopidae. Most living members of these families are small, delicate, wormlike burrowing creatures. The oldest known identifiable Scolecophidia fossil was found in Europe and dates to the early Eocene epoch. During the Eocene, which lasted from 55 to 36 million years ago, boids became the dominant snake group. Members of the superfamily Colubroidea evolved during the early Eocene, perhaps as much as 55 million years ago. This group gave rise to the modern colubrids, the dominant snake family in the world today.

The Oligocene epoch began 36 million years ago and ended 22.5 million years ago. The few snake fossils from this epoch were found in Europe and North America. The most important event in snake evolution during the Oligocene is the appearance of the first members of the family Colubridae, the dominant modern snakes. Colubrid fossils that are between 30 and 32 million years of age have been found both in Europe and North America, strongly suggesting that migration of species led to colubrids of approximately the same age being found in two different localities. Where colubrids evolved is unknown. It is possible they initially evolved in Eurasia and thence moved westward to North America, although certainly other scenarios, such

Boa constrictor: Boas and their relatives, the pythons, have been successful, populating areas throughout the world.

as an initial evolution in Asia and movement into North America via the Bering land bridge, cannot be discounted. In the early Miocene epoch, 25 million years ago, Africa and Eurasia, which had been separated for millions of years, came into contact again. This allowed for dispersal of colubroids and boids into Africa.

Interestingly, most snake fossils have been found in either western Europe or western North America. The snake fossil record for the other continents is negligible, so much of our information on locations of snake evolution is conjectural.

What we do know is that there was a radiation, or increase, in the number of colubroid species, especially the colubrids, during this time, 22.5 to 5.5 million years ago. The venomous elapids and viperids, both of colubroid stock, first appeared during the early Miocene. The colubroids became the dominant form of snake life present on earth and have remained so through to the present. Some of the modern-day snakes of all families are seen

The south African glossy worm snake, *Leptotyphlops scutifrons*. Adults may grow to 9 to 10 inches (225 to 250 mm).

© John Visser

beginning in the Pliocene, 1.8 to 5.5 million years ago, when the continents looked pretty much as they do today.

Thus from their humble beginnings about 140 million years ago, as what may have been burrowing creatures, snakes have diversified to approximately 2,700 species in fifteen families. Some snakes, such as the Scolecophidia, live a secretive existence underground, burrowing as they go. Others, such as the marine elapids or venomous sea snakes, live in the oceans, traveling from continent to continent. Some, such as the tree boa, are arboreal, living in trees. But most snakes spend most of their lives on the ground, eating small animals that happen to pass by. These modern snake species are only, at most, five or so millions of years old, probably twice the age of humanity. But they reflect more than 100 million years of evolutionary change and geographic distribution and redistribution. We will explore some of their unique adaptations in the ensuing chapters.

Leptotyphlops nigricans, another African burrowing snake.

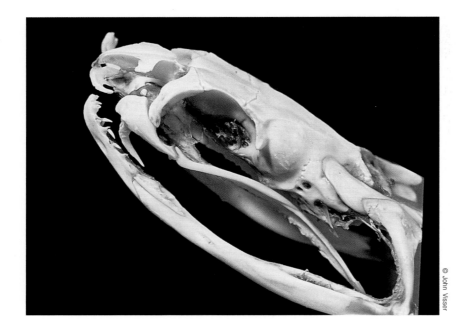

Skull of the cape cobra, *Naja nivea*. Notice the fang on the maxillary bone and the inward curving teeth on the dentate bone of the lower jaw.

© John Visser

*I*n fossil snakes, the structure and shape of the vertebrae are the most important characteristics used for classification; in living snakes, the entire snake is available for study. Taxonomists who classify living snakes examine structural features and, more recently, have been using biochemical tests. Some of these structural features include skull morphology, or the structure of the skull; the structure and connection of muscle to bone, especially the long muscles of the back; and the presence or absence of pelvic bones. One of the most unique ways to classify snakes is according to the structure of the male's copulatory organ, or hemipenes. Male snakes have two penes, erroneously called a hemipenis, as if each were half of one

functional organ. The hemipenes are inverted within the tail of the snake, one on each side of the sexual and excretory opening, which is called the vent. When used in copulation, one hemipenis is everted, like a glove being turned inside out, by a hydraulic system that pumps fluid into the hemipenis. Snake taxonomists often classify snakes according to the shape, size, and structure of the hemipenis. Hemipenes are grooved and may have numerous spikes, cuplike structures, bumps, and other ornamentation, much of it used to keep the hemipenis within the female's cloaca during copulation. By looking at similarities and differences between hemipenes, it is possible to classify living snakes. One of the drawbacks, of course, is that you

must have the male specimen in order to classify it.

Snake taxonomists also use other characteristics to classify snakes, including numbers and arrangement of scale rows and structure of teeth. Since the 1980s, scientists have been looking at immunological differences between the serum proteins and venoms of snakes to determine the relationships between them. More modern techniques use DNA fingerprinting in which DNA (deoxyribonucleic acid), the genetic material, is extracted from the cells of the snakes in question and compared in order to establish whether a relationship exists. DNA fingerprinting is still a relatively new technique in snake taxonomy.

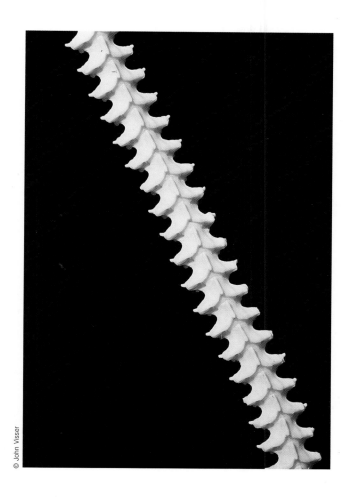

© John Visser

Vertebral column of a South African spotted house snake, *Lamprophis guttatus*. The connections between adjacent vertebrae allow the snake to move sideways without dislocating its backbone.

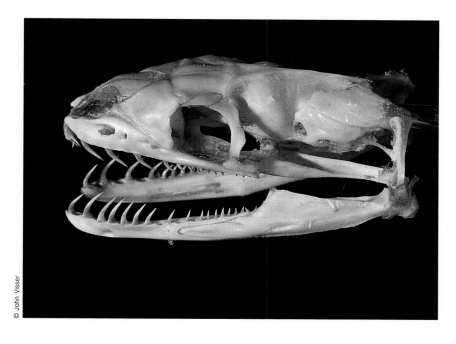

© John Visser

Python's skull: A full complement of recurved teeth on the upper and lower jaws prevents prey, once grabbed, from pulling out of the python's mouth.

Classification of the Boa Constrictor

Kingdom	Animalia: animals
Phylum	Chordata: chordates with notochords
Subphylum	Vertebrata: vertebrates
Class	Reptilia: reptiles
Order	Squamata: lizards, ringed lizards, and snakes
Suborder	Serpentes: snakes
Infraorder	Alethinophidia: most snakes
Superfamily	Booidea
Family	Boidae: the boids (BOW-ids)
Subfamily	Boinae
Genus	*Boa*
Species	*Boa constrictor*

Families of Living Snakes

Infraorder Scolecophidia—small, burrowing snakes
  Family Anomolepididae—small Central and South American burrowing snakes
  Family Typhlopidae—burrowing snakes, worldwide distribution
  Family Leptotyphlopidae—small, blind, burrowing snakes, also called thread snakes, found in Africa, Asia, and North and South America

Infraorder Alethinophidia
Superfamily Acrochordoidea
  Family Acrochordidae—wart snakes or elephant trunk snakes
Superfamily Anilioidea
  Family Loxocemidae—*Loxocemus*, South Mexico and Central America
  Family Xenopeltidae—sunbeam snake, Southeast Asia
  Family Aniliidae—burrowing snakes, *Anilius* of South America
  Family Uropeltidae
    Subfamily Cylindropheinae—Southeast Asian burrowing snakes
    Subfamily Uropeltinae—shield-tailed burrowing snakes from India and Sri Lanka
Superfamily Tropidopheoidea
    Subfamily Ungaliopheinae—dwarf boas from the tropical New World
    Subfamily Tropidopheinae—wood snakes with tracheal lung from the tropical New World
Superfamily Bolyeroidea—Round Island snakes
  Family Bolyeriidae—Round Island snakes
Superfamily Booidea
  Family Pythonidae—pythons—Asia, Africa, and Australia
  Family Boidae—viviparous, bearing live young, from the New World, the Pacific, Malagasy, Africa, and Eurasia
    Subfamily Boinae—the boas
    Subfamily Erycinae—semi-burrowing boas, North America and Old World
Superfamily Colubroidea*
  Family Colubridae—most modern snakes, worldwide distribution, some venomous with rear fangs that are grooved
  Family Atractaspididae—burrowing venomous snakes, Africa and the Middle East
  Family Elapidae—venomous with nonretractable fangs with canals for venom injection, worldwide distribution
  Family Viperidae—venomous with retractable fangs with enclosed canal for venom injection
    Subfamily Azemiopinae—Fea's viper *Azemiops*, Southeast Asia
    Subfamily Crotalinae—pit vipers from Asia, Eastern Europe, and the New World
    Subfamily Viperinae—true vipers from Africa and Eurasia

*Colubridae and Elapidae have numerous subfamilies.
(Following Samuel McDowell, 1987, and John Cadle, 1987)

chapter two

FORM AND FUNCTION

© Rom Whitaker

*I*t is not possible to understand the behavior of snakes without first taking a look at their form and learning how that form works to enable them to act as they do. By simply looking at a snake's body, we can glean some information about how it lives, the temperatures it may be exposed to, the manner by which it acquires food, and some idea of what that food may be. Its form may also give us insights into some of its basic behavior patterns.

Snakes have a well-developed skeleton, with a long backbone and many ribs. They lack forelimbs, shoulder bones, a collarbone, and a breastbone, although the boas, pythons, and a few other snakes from the oldest lineages have rudimentary hind legs and a pelvic girdle. A breastbone could restrict the maximum diameter of the body. The lack of one allows for the passage of very large food items. This is a great advantage to an animal that only eats other animals and cannot chew or break up its food into small pieces. Snake teeth are well designed for eating large animals whole. Needlelike, sharp, and pointed, the fishhook-like recurved teeth point toward the rear of the snake's throat and pierce prey easily. With most snakes having more than 200 teeth, no amount of struggling enables the prey, once caught, to escape the grasp of the jaws. A snake's teeth are continually shed, in one of nature's best maintenance programs, and are replaced with new teeth before the older teeth loosen and fall out.

Snakes also lack movable eyelids to cover their eyes. Thus, snake eyes are always open but are covered by a layer of transparent skin that is replaced when the snake sheds its skin. Although snakes have some internal ear structures, they lack external ear openings.

Unlike mammals, including humans and birds, reptiles are ectotherms. That is, they cannot maintain a stable body temperature by internal mechanisms and must rely on the environmental temperatures around them to maintain their own body temperatures at functional levels. A snake's life revolves around methods to warm or cool its body. Every bodily function and behavior is affected by the temperature of the snake's body. Each species has a preferred or optimum range of temperatures it requires to feed, breed, and metabolize its food. It also has critical temperature limits at which exposure for any appreciable period of time will result in death. For most species, exposure to a high temperature of 110°F (44°C) or a low temperature of about 35°F (2°C) can be fatal.

The Gaboon viper, *Bitis gabonica*, a venomous viperine of Africa, eating a mouse. Injection of venom kills the mouse and begins the digestive process. All snakes preferentially eat their prey head first, both preventing bites to the snake and preventing the prey's limbs from becoming stuck in the snake's esophagus.

© John Visser

The African egg-eating snake, *Dasypeltis* species. Sharp projections from the backbone slit the egg so the contents can travel down the digestive tract. The shell is regurgitated.

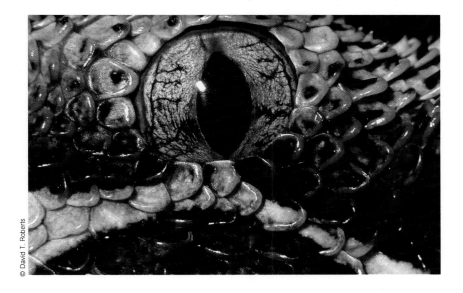

© David T. Roberts

A snake's eye. Notice the lack of movable eyelids.

© John Visser

Scales of the green mamba, *Dendroaspis viridis*, an elapid. Larger scales are on the belly, smaller ones on the sides. Their scales are adaptations for climbing trees.

Each species has evolved with the best combination of body form, covering of scales, and musculature to enable it to move about in a way that allows it to find and secure food, defend itself, change its body temperature, and reproduce in its particular habitat or ecological niche.

The boa constrictor, *Boa constrictor*, has small, smooth scales of equal size all over its upper body. It does some climbing.

Snakes have many extremely movable ribs that are attached to the vertebral column and to each other with elastic muscles and tendons. They are also attached to the skin by connecting muscles. The skin contains other connecting muscles. Not only can the snake control the movements of its ribs and skin, but the movements of its individual scales as well. As a result, snakes have the ability to modify all of their body movements to accommodate different surroundings and terrain. Obviously, as snakes do not have any functional limbs to propel themselves, they must use their ability to push against nearby objects or surface irregularities in order to move forward. (The short rudimentary hind legs that terminate in a sharp spur on pythons and boas are only useful in courtship and have no ability to move the snake.) Alternatively, some arboreal constricting snakes are able to anchor part of their body by forming a grasp of coils around one object, such as a branch or twig, and then reach to the next object for another anchoring point. This form of locomotion is called "hitch and hike" and is used in climbing.

The rock rattlesnake, *Crotalus lepidus*, of the southwestern United States and Mexico. Rattlesnakes have heavily keeled scales and well-camouflaged patterns.

Sidewinding, where movement forward is accomplished by moving
sideways.

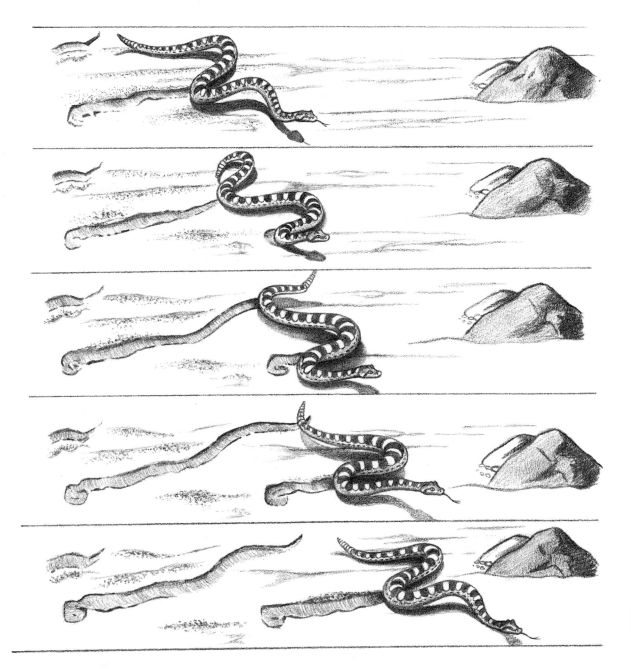

BODY FORM

Snakes have several basic body types, each designed for living in different ways. Think of snakes as flexible tubes, some long and thin, some thick and fat, with the contents or internal organs arranged to fit the cylindrical housing and covered with a protective material that can be nimbly manipulated from within and has a surface texture that provides contacts with its surroundings.

Slender bodies

Slender bodies have evolved for species that need to move quickly. Whether they need to move rapidly on land or in the treetops, the advantages of slender body forms are the same. Fleet terrestrial snakes, such as the racers and whipsnakes of the family Colubridae, have long, streamlined bodies and frequently have smooth scales that enable them to glide swiftly over the ground and through dense underbrush. The deadly black mamba *Dendroaspis polylepis* of Africa is an example of a fleet slender-bodied terrestrial snake.

The African black mamba, *Dendroaspis polylepis*, is a thin-bodied terrestrial species. Other mambas are highly arboreal and climb well.

© Johan Marais

Snakes that live in the upper levels of bushes and trees, such as the vine snakes, are generally long and slender as well. Their streamlined shape carries a low body weight, allowing the animal to pass over thin twigs and branches without breaking them. Thinner snakes can traverse the finest outermost branches. Such snakes progress by simply using body contact to push against the twigs, leaves, and branches over which they pass. Slender arboreal species often have one or two ridges on the scales on each side of the belly that run the length of the body, which help the snake hold on to branches. One of the most unique of the arboreal species possessing belly ridges is the flying snake *Chrysopelia* of Southeast Asia. Highly muscular, this colubrid can also flatten its slender body and glide from upper to lower branches like a ribbon. Most slender-bodied snakes find themselves virtually helpless and unable to progress at all on smooth surfaces that lack something to push against.

The African boomslang, *Dispholidus typus*, one of the few venomous colubrids. Its body is long and slender.

While some slender-bodied arboreal species lack extensive body musculature, others, like the tree boas of the genus *Corallus* of South America, are true constrictors that use their powerful body muscles to throw a "hitch" of coils around a branch and "hike" themselves up as they climb. They frequently capture their prey by anchoring their muscular body and prehensile tail to a branch, which then enables them to make long strikes to capture birds in flight or other animals climbing on nearby branches. They hunt by moving slowly from branch to branch and waiting for prey to come within reach.

Candoia carinata, one of the Pacific Island boas from New Guinea, the Solomon Islands, and other islands in the southern Pacific. This is a moderate-bodied snake.

Stout-bodied snakes are not suited for climbing. They are best adapted for traveling on the surface of the ground. Wide short bodies, heavy weight, and wide belly scales provide the optimal surface contact for travel over different types of terrain. While stout-bodied snakes may use undulating body movements to push against nearby objects and ground irregularities, they can also use a caterpillar-like action to move forward. The body remains in a straight line, while the ribs and individual belly scales move in a progressive action similar to the movements of a caterpillar, picking up and laying down one row of belly scales after another. The track that is left behind is nearly a straight line depression in the soil, as wide as the snake's body. This method of progression is often used by the Gaboon viper *Bitis gabonica* of Africa and a number of short, stout ground pythons, such as the blood python *Python curtus* of Southeast Asia.

The Gaboon viper, *Bitis gabonica*, a stout-bodied viperine. The large head holds a massive venom gland apparatus that produces copious amounts of highly toxic venom.

The blood python, *Python curtur*, of
Malaysia, Borneo and Sumatra, is a
terrestrial and semi-aquatic species
that resides in tropical rain forests.

Moderate bodies

Most of the world's snakes fall into this broad category. It includes venomous and nonvenomous snakes, giant constricting snakes, and small ground and aquatic snakes. Some ground and burrowing species have moderate cylindrical bodies with absolutely smooth scales covering them. This includes some members of the families Typhlopidae and Leptotyphlopidae.

© John Visser

Above: The glass smooth scales and shovel-like snout on a head that is as big around as the body makes this blind snake (*Typhlops schlegelii*) a well-adapted digging machine.

Opposite: The iridescent metallic blue colors that reflect from the smooth scales of the Brazilian rainbow boa, *Epicrates c. cenchria*, give this nocturnal species its name.

INTERNAL ANATOMY

The snake's elongated cylindrical body does not permit the usual vertebrate internal anatomy. Organs that are paired in other vertebrates, such as lungs, kidneys, ovaries, and testes, must be reduced or rearranged in snakes.

Most snakes have one right lung. In those with a left lung, it may be reduced, as in boids and pythons, or vestigial and non-functional. Or it may be entirely lost. The lung may be very long, in some cases reaching almost to the vent or cloacal opening. Some snakes have developed a tracheal lung overlying and within the trachea, which augments the functioning of the true lung. Snakes do not have a muscular diaphragm, and breathing is accomplished by muscular contractions that move the ribs, expanding and contracting the closed body cavity that contains the lung and the other internal organs.

Snake kidneys are greatly elongated, and the right kidney tends to be placed more rostrally, or more toward the head of the snake, than the left kidney. Snakes do not require a urinary bladder, because the waste is semi-solid. Gonads may be elongated, one placed more toward the head than the other, and the female may lack an oviduct on the left side.

The alimentary canal or digestive tube is also modified. The stomach is simply an elongated thickened area at the base of the esophagus. The small intestine is moderately coiled but the large intestine is straight. The accessory organs of digestion—the gall-bladder, liver, and spleen—are placed more toward the head than in most other vertebrates, and the liver is elongated and very far forward.

The snake's heart is not significantly different from that of other reptiles except for the crocodilians. It is functionally three-chambered. There is a fourth chamber, but it is not completely separated from the third. Oxygenated blood from the lungs mixes with deoxygenated blood being returned from the general circulation. Thus, the three-chambered heart is less efficient than the four-chambered heart found in crocodilians, birds, and mammals in which only oxygenated blood is pumped back into the general circulation.

As already mentioned, shoulder and pelvic girdles are absent in most snakes. The Booidea maintain rudimentary pelvic bones, and several other snakes also have some remnants of a pelvis. The Leptotyphlopidae are unique in that they also have a rudimentary femur in the area of the vent.

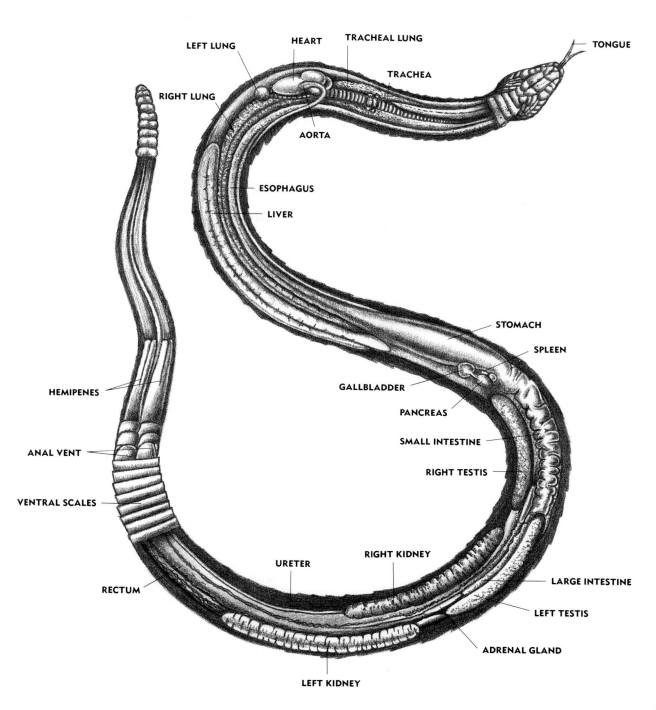

LEFT LUNG

HEART

TRACHEAL LUNG

TRACHEA

TONGUE

RIGHT LUNG

AORTA

ESOPHAGUS

LIVER

STOMACH

SPLEEN

GALLBLADDER

PANCREAS

SMALL INTESTINE

RIGHT TESTIS

HEMIPENES

ANAL VENT

VENTRAL SCALES

RECTUM

URETER

RIGHT KIDNEY

LARGE INTESTINE

LEFT TESTIS

ADRENAL GLAND

LEFT KIDNEY

© Pat Ortega

snake anatomy

Opposite: Many vipers (Family: Viperidae) have keeled, rough scales.

Unlike amphibians, whose scaleless skin must remain moist, snakes have a skin that acts as a waterproof coat and protects the body. Snakes are covered with scales in a variety of shapes, arrangements, and textures. Scale size varies by family and species. Boas and pythons have tiny scales in large numbers of rows while many of the racers and whipsnakes have large scales in few rows. While the scales of some snakes are glass smooth, others are coarse and may have one or several keel-like ridges that may align from scale to scale to form longer ridges that run the length of the snake's body, giving the snake a rough appearance. Many of the vipers have large, heavily keeled scales, while most of the elapids have smooth scales. Saw-scaled vipers, *Echis carinatus*,

The green tree python, *Chondropython viridis*, has satiny smooth scales. When the snake lies draped on a branch, rainwater collects in the body folds and drips down to the head, enabling the snake to drink.

Boas (Family: Boidae) have numerous small, relatively smooth scales.

The raised scales of the African rough-scaled or "hairy" viper, *Atheris hispidus*, obscure its shape as it blends into the green foliage. Colors range from green to yellow and black.

© David T. Roberts

© David T. Roberts

Hidden under the sand with only its eyes visible, this McMahon's viper, *Eristocophis macmahoni*, is virtually undetectable as it lies in wait for prey and protects itself from the hot sun.

have keeled scales that they can rub together to produce a buzzing sound. Some snakes have scales that include what are believed to be sensory pits as well. The elephant trunk snake, *Achrochordus javanicus*, has small diamond-shaped scales that have raised sharp tubercles, giving the snake the feel of a rasp file. It uses the pointed scales to grasp fish in a quick fold of its body.

Most snakes have scales that are like overlapping pointed shingles on a roof while others, like a number of sea snakes, have hexagonal scales that fit side by side without overlapping. Most snake scales lie in oblique (diagonal) rows that meet at the apex of the back at the midline. The Middle Eastern leaf-nosed viper, *Eristocophis macmahoni*, has scales that are teardrop in shape, keeled, and lie in extremely oblique rows on the sides of the body. By manipulating its body and individual scales, it can literally sink out of sight by using the scales to throw sand over its back to cover itself. Scientists have only begun to look at the snake skin and the array of coloration, texture, and sensitivity it possesses.

It is easy to understand that a body covering that receives the wear that a snake skin does would need to be repaired or replaced regularly. Snakes do this by shedding their skin periodically, a process called ecdysis. The frequency of shedding depends on a number of factors. Young snakes are growing rapidly and need to renew their skins often. Old snakes shed infrequently. Damage to the skin will prompt a snake to repair the damage and shed.

The elephant trunk snakes, *Acrochordus* species, are aquatic snakes that have numerous small, pointed, raised scales that help grip the fish that the snake seizes in a quick clench of its body folds.

© Rom Whitaker

Snakes that develop skin infections often shed continually. Some species, such as the Indigo snake, *Drymarchon corais*, shed as frequently as every twenty-two days, while boas and pythons may shed only once in several months.

The process of shedding takes about two weeks. As the time for shedding approaches, the snake often begins to fast. The eyes become milky white and the skin becomes dull as a lymphlike fluid separates the old outer layer of skin from the new skin underneath. Nearly blind, the snake remains quiet and hidden in a moist retreat. About ten days later the eyes clear. The snake begins to shed about three days after that. Should the new skin become damaged before it is ready to take the place of the outer skin, a scar will result. The snake begins shedding by rubbing its skin against a rough surface, which loosens it around the mouth and nose. As the skin begins to come away, the snake continues to drag itself over rough objects, pushing the skin from the mouth back over its head. Slowly the snake crawls out through the "mouth" of the shedding skin. Each scale of the body moves to separate itself and release the old skin, leaving it behind like an inverted glove.

This red-tailed rat snake, *Gonyosoma oxycephala*, has just begun to shed. Even the skin covering the eyes is cast off. The shed is a duplicate of the snake's scalation and found "sheds" can be used to identify the species to which the skin belonged.

SNAKE TAILS

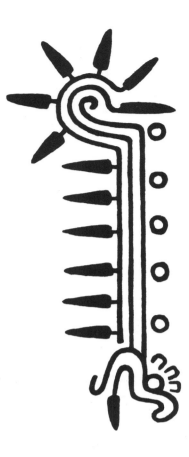

Most snakes have rather nondescript cylindrical tails, although there is a distinct difference in tail length and shape between males and females. Because the male copulatory organs, or hemipenes, lie inverted inside the base of the tail, males generally have tails that are thicker at the base. Females, on the other hand, have tails that taper gradually to the end. The vipers in particular show a dramatic sexual dimorphism, with the tail of the female short and narrow, barely a third the length of a male's and not nearly as thick.

Many species of burrowing and ground snakes have tails that end in a blunt rounded end, as though the body were abruptly cut off. Sometimes the blunt tail is colored to resemble the head, such as in the Asian sand boa *Eryx johnii*. The snake may even hide its true head when disturbed and hold the tail obviously high to fool an attacker into seizing the less vulnerable body part. Some species of burrowing fossorial snakes have a blunt tail that terminates in sharp spines. These are the shield-tail snakes, *Uropeltis*, which use the tail spines to anchor themselves within their burrows as they press the body forward to dig with their head. The spines are also used to create an impenetrable door, blocking off the burrow to intruders.

Arboreal species and swift terrestrial snakes often have very long slender tails that are consistent with their streamlined body shape. The Gold's tree cobra, *Pseudohaje goldi*, of West Africa, well known for its incredible ability to move at great speed through the treetops, has a tail that is about a third of the length of the slender body.

Arboreal constrictors are able to use their long prehensile tails to anchor the body and strike out at prey for nearly the entire length of the body, as opposed to about a third of the body length used for striking by most snakes. This is a great feeding advantage where prey must be captured at considerable distances or even on the wing. On the other hand, the small aquatic tentacled snake, *Erpeton tentaculatum*, uses its prehensile tail to grasp the aquatic plants it lives in as a way of stabilizing its body in a relatively vertical position.

The most unique and well known of all tail appendages is that of the New World rattlesnakes. Baby rattlesnakes are born with a hard keratinized blunt "prebutton" at the end of the tail. Soon after birth, the snake finishes its first shedding, loses the prebutton in the process, and begins to build a rattle with a first rattle segment or "button." New rings of dried keratinized skin remain after each subsequent shedding and separate the original terminal button from the actual end of the tail vertebrae. The rings of dried skin segments fit inside each other much like taking a series of clothing snap fasteners and snapping them one inside the other to form a flexible series of segments. One cannot tell the age of a rattlesnake by the number of segments composing its rattle. As the snake adds a ring each time it sheds, the number of segments indicate the number of sheds the snake has experienced. As a rattlesnake sheds between three and five times a year, it can build quite a long string of rattles. Young adult snakes have the longest rattles because they are fast growing and shed often. As they age, the rattle has more time to abrade against objects the snake crawls through and over and so the end rattle segments tend to be lost. Thus, very old snakes generally have very few rattle segments. It is not unusual for "snake show" entertainers to snap together the rattle segments from several rattlesnakes in order to make an unbelievably long rattle on one snake, as testimonial that it is the "oldest rattlesnake in the world." When the snake vibrates its tail rapidly in annoyance, the loose-fitting rings of skin rasp against each other and produce a buzzing sound or "rattle" that is unmistakable and can be heard for several yards (meters). The snake can vary the speed of its rattle and the sound, depending on the degree of annoyance it is experiencing and the temperature of the snake. Often after a period of extreme annoyance, the buzz may taper off to little more than a number of random clicks.

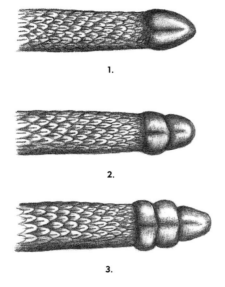

1.

2.

3.

4.

5.

Snakes generally live to be eighteen to twenty-five years old and mature at four to six years of age. Although you cannot tell the age of a rattlesnake by the segments of the rattle, you can presume that a rattle containing only a button is from a newborn (see illustrations 1 and 2), containing two or three segments and a button is probably from a snake a year or two old (illustration 3), a number of segments still with the original button is a young adult (illustration 4), and a short rattle with worn sides and no terminal end (illustration 5) is an adult well on in years. Opposite: Prairie rattlesnake, *Crotalus viridis*.

Most species of snakes vibrate their tails when annoyed, but lacking a rattle, they do not produce a noise. However, many a hiker in the northeastern United States has bolted in alarm at the "rattling" buzz produced by the harmless black racer, *Coluber constrictor*, when it vibrates its long, slender tail among fallen dead leaves.

While round tails are adequate for travel on and under the land and in trees, they do not work very well in the open sea. The sea snakes therefore are characterized by a distinctly paddle-shaped tail that they use to stabilize and change their swimming direction. The sea snakes use the same undulating body movement that land snakes do for propulsion, pushing against water instead of a firm object.

HEAD SHAPES

While some snakes have heads that are indistinguishable in shape from the body and neck, like the coral snakes, *Micrurus*, burrowing viper, *Atractaspis*, and burrowing python, *Calabaria*, other species have heads that are broad and triangle shaped, quite distinct from the neck and body. Such a shape is generally associated with the vipers and other stout or moderately bodied venomous snakes. The enlarged head accommodates long fangs and large venom-producing glands located at the base of the skull.

This cantil, *Agkistrodon bilineatus*, a pit viper, has a wide heart-shaped head and can produce large quantities of potent venom. However, many harmless beneficial snakes have large heads as well.

However, many species of harmless snakes also have large heads, like the water snakes, *Nerodia*, of the southeastern United States. Some snakes can flatten the head extensively when annoyed. Broad or moderate-shaped heads in most species simply can accommodate rotund larger prey. The hognose snake is sometimes called the "hissing adder" because of its large viperlike head and stout body. It feeds on toads, which inflate themselves like little balloons as they are eaten, so a big head and body on the snake offers advantages. Some long-bodied rear-fanged species of relatively "harmless" colubrids have broad viperlike heads as well, such as the Asian and African species of *Boiga*.

© John Visser

Although its wide head suggests the shape of a viper, the nonvenomous green tree python, *Chondropython viridis*, also has a blunt nose, large eyes, and heat-sensing pits on its upper lips. The large head enables it to eat bulky birds and rats.

© David T. Roberts

With a snout that tapers to a fine point to resemble the end of a leaf, the vine snake, *Oxybelis fulgidus*, sways gently, looking and acting like a harmless vine in the wind to fool lizards, its agile, quick prey.

Conversely, some of the deadliest of venomous snakes, the Elapidae, have small, streamlined heads, including the Australian taipan, *Oxyuranus scutellatus*. The fangs are also small, as are the venom glands, which produce small quantities of highly toxic and very efficient venom. Streamlined slender snakes, particularly arboreal species, often have narrow, pointed heads to complete the body form. Many of these species have diffuse venom glands that have little mass and secrete poison at the base of a few grooved and slightly enlarged teeth on the rear of the upper jaw.

Many snakes sport head appendages that serve specific functions. Burrowing species often have flattened shovel-like snouts for digging, such as the North American western shovel-nosed snake, *Chionactis occipitalis*; upturned snouts for shoveling soil, such as the hognosed snakes, *Heterodon*; or blunt, rounded heads for pushing and moving through tunnels and soil, like the North American rubber boa, *Charina bottae*. Snakes that use soft soils for concealment, lying just under the surface, sometimes have peculiar appendages whose purpose is unclear. The leaf-nosed snake of the Middle East, *Eristocophis macmahoni*, has mustachelike projections stemming sideways from the tip of its snout, while desert horned vipers, *Cerastes cerastes*, have pointed projections over each eye. Some arboreal species, particularly vine snakes such as *Oxybelis*, *Dryophis*, and *Ahaetulla*, have long, pointed snouts. The leaf-nosed vine snake, *Ahaetulla*, goes even further with a leaflike projection that completes its camouflage.

It is apparent that snakes are unique in their physical forms, which provide both advantages and disadvantages for survival. However, it is not until we combine these forms with the wonderful sensory mechanisms snakes have developed and the behavioral patterns that have emerged that we can fully appreciate the success of these intriguing animals.

The pointed snout and small head of the burrowing viper, *Atractaspis engaddensis*, give no hint of the large folded fangs or the potent venom glands that extend from the head into the neck. Although called vipers, members of the genus *Atractaspis* are classified in their own family, not the viperids.

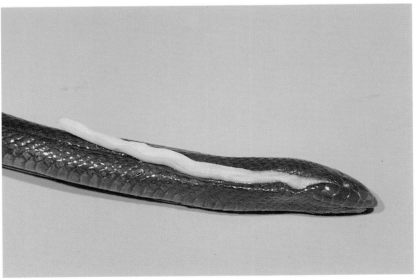

© Johan Marais

The hornlike scales on the snout of the intricately colored rhinoceros viper, *Bitis nasicornis*, give the snake its name. Their benefit to this highly venomous, water-loving species is unclear.

© David T. Roberts

Likewise unclear is the use of the prominent hornlike projections over the eye of the desert horned viper, *Cerastes cerastes*. They remain exposed as the snake lies buried in the sand. A natural trip device?

chapter three

SENSES

© Rom Whitaker

Watch a hungry snake strike a live mouse. With absolute accuracy, the snake aims and strikes. Rarely does a snake miss. This behavior is made possible by an extremely sensitive and highly adapted sensory system.

VISION

Visual stimulation is one of the cues used by snakes to determine the presence and location of prey. But vision in snakes varies from taxonomic family to taxonomic family. Most of the fossorial snakes, such as the primitive, and ancient, burrowing Scolecophidia, have reduced eyes or may not appear to have any eyes at all. Eyes on some of these snakes may be no more than darkened spots under a thick scale. Vision in some of these burrowers may be limited to light perception. Less primitive terrestrial and aquatic snakes need to see to search for food, capture prey, identify enemies, mate, and travel. Thus, for these animals, differentiation between light and dark is not enough.

The milky eyes of this garter snake, *Thamnophis sirtalis*, herald the renewing of its skin in the shedding process called ecdysis, which takes about ten days to complete.

If you have a pet snake, you will notice that before shedding, its eyes, which are covered by a layer of skin called the brille, or the spectacle, become opaque. During this time, the snake will not feed, probably, in part, due to its inability to clearly see the food. (As snakes are carnivorous, in the wild the food would be live prey.) Immediately prior to shedding, the eyes clear due to complete separation between the underlying new skin and overlying old skin, and the snake again can see clearly. If, as sometimes occurs, eye skin or "caps" remain on the eyes after shedding, the caps will build up after several shedding cycles and the animal will refuse food—probably partly because the animal cannot see the food. This is further proof that vision is essential to many species of snakes, particularly diurnal (active during the day) species, for feeding.

Snakes have unique eyes among the Reptilia. Most higher vertebrates have a fovea centralis, an indentation within the retina that is the region of most acute vision where images are in clear focus. Most snakes lack foveas. Two genera of colubrids have foveas, but their eyes are very specialized. In other reptiles, birds, and mammals, accommodation, or changing from distant to near vision, results from contraction of ciliary muscles that cause deformation of the lens. Humans, too, have flexible lenses, which we become acutely aware of as we age and find that the flexibility is decreased and we must wear reading glasses. Snakes have no ciliary muscles, and accommodation results from contraction of the iris, the pigmented portion of the eye. This contraction leads to increased pressure in the posterior chamber of the eye, which is filled with a gelantinous fluid called vitreous fluid or the vitreous body. The increased pressure, in turn, pushes the lens into the eye's anterior chamber, which changes the position of the lens and bends the light.

The shape of the pupil, the opening in the center of the iris that allows light to enter into the eye, suggests whether the snake is diurnal, active during the day, or nocturnal, active at night. Diurnal snakes often have round or horizontal pupils, and nocturnal snakes tend to have elliptical pupils. The elliptical pupils can open wider than round ones, allowing more light into the eye at night than round pupils. This adaptation to nocturnal or crepuscular behavior is seen in many species. Cats and crocodilians are the more familiar examples. People sometimes mistakenly attribute malevolence to the slit-eyed stare of crotalids, the common pit vipers in the United States. Crotalids are mostly nocturnal and need to gather as much light as possible into their eyes during their post-sunset hunting forays.

A diamondback water snake, below, *Nerodia rhombifera*, scans the aquatic plants for unsuspecting frogs. Agile swimmers, they are adept at hunting by night or day. The bamboo viper, bottom, *Trimeresurus* species, has an elliptical pupil, which is typical for many nocturnal snakes and vipers.

The eyes of snakes are located on the sides of the head. This positioning allows for a good lateral view of their surroundings but not very much forward or binocular (using both eyes) vision. Snakes tend to have an extremely narrow field of binocular vision, not more than about twenty degrees. In most species, the definition of stationary, or non-moving, objects appears to be less well developed than the ability to perceive movement. Thus a snake is apt to crawl right past prey it is pursuing if the prey suddenly stops and remains motionless. Vine snakes, which feed on highly camouflaged and often motionless lizards and frogs, would be at a particular disadvantage with such a poor system of visualization. To correct the problem, some vine snakes, such as in the genus *Ahaetulla*, appear to have developed a greater degree of binocular vision. Vision is further enhanced by the eyes being rotated slightly forward rather than on the sides of the head. There is a depression on each side of the snout in front of the eyes that more or less gets the elongated pointed snout out of the snake's line of sight and increases its forward vision. The eyes are large, as in many arboreal species, but differ from those of most snakes in having a horizontal keyhole-shaped pupil that gathers more light to produce a better image. These snakes also have foveas and the binocular system works to focus the image directly on the fovea.

The eyes of the diurnal arboreal boomslang, *Dispholidus typus*, are a slightly different example. The boomslang's eyes have very large, round pupils and are set high on the side of its head. Instead of being rotated forward, the eyes are so large that their curvature includes a forward aspect, giving the snake a very wide field of vision. This snake is particularly adapted for spotting

The large eyes of the African boom-slang, *Dispholidus typus*, are classic examples of eyes in a strictly diurnal species. The movement of any prey is quickly noticed and the prey attacked.

© John Visser

birds, which it quickly strikes out at and seizes as they momentarily land or fly by.

Color vision in snakes depends upon whether the snake is nocturnal or diurnal. Nocturnal snakes have no need for color vision as there is not enough light available at night to see colors. Therefore, they have retinas that are composed entirely of rods, light-sensitive cells that allow an image to be produced in the absence of color vision. Many nocturnal animals have such eyes, which reflect light and give the impression of glowing in the dark like hot coals when light is shined into them. At night, we humans use the rods as our primary vision system, giving us a colorless, shadowy view of our environments. Animals with only rods in their eyes can see in light, but they cannot see color, so having a rod-only eye does not preclude daytime activity. And, in fact, many nocturnal snakes tending to hunt at night, such as the crotalids, or pit vipers, are out basking in the sun during the day.

Many diurnal colubrids have unique cone-only eyes. Cones are receptors that are specialized for color vision. Humans, for example, have cones specialized for stimulation in red, green, and blue wavelengths. Diurnal snakes may even have "double cones," which can receive stimulation for two colors. The problem for diurnal snakes with cone-only eyes is that they cannot see at all at night, as cones are specialized exclusively for color vision, which occurs only in light. Although rod-only eyes are well known among nocturnal animals (however, there is more and more evidence that nocturnal mammals, thought to have rod-only eyes, also have cones), diurnal animals, with humans being a prime example, tend to have both rods and cones in the eyes. The absence of rods in eyes of some colubrids limits the snakes' activities to daytime. Most diurnal snakes, however, have taken a more conservative evolutionary approach and have both rods and cones in their eyes.

Some scientists have suggested that the differences between the snake's eyes and the eyes of other reptiles is a result of the initial evolution of snakes as burrowing animals with reduced eyes. Eyes would have been reduced due to both lack of need of vision within the dark burrows and necessary protection of eyes against abrasion while burrowing. Thus, the modern snake eye would have had to reevolve from the remnants of eyes in the ancient burrowers. You may, however, remember from the chapter on evolution that snake fossils are few and far between, and therefore, what we do not know about snake evolution far exceeds what we do know or suspect. Furthermore, other scientists, such as Jean-Claude Rage of the Université Pierre et Marie Curie in Paris, have suggested that rather than burrowing, some of the earlier snakes may have had a secretive mode of life, which may have led to evolution of these distinctive characteristics of the visual system. This, in a way, makes more sense than assuming that in evolution snakes lost most of their visual abilities and then reevolved eyes that are somewhat different from, but distinctly similar to, eyes in the mainstream of vertebrate development.

Diurnal snakes have a yellow lens. This again is a unique adaptation in snakes as most animals have clear, unpigmented lenses. The yellow, as anyone who has worn yellow sunglasses knows, filters out blue light, increases contrast, and makes it easier to see moving animals.

Snake eyes are lidless and cannot be closed. During sleep, snakes with elliptical pupils almost imperceptibly cant their pupils downward.

Snakes have no tear glands, but the Harderian gland in the eye produces an oily secretion that lubricates the cornea under the brille and is drained via the tear ducts, which lead to the area around Jacobson's organ.

Although it is said that snakes cannot move their eyes, they have a full complement of oculomotor muscles, the muscles attached to the eyeball responsible for eye movement. In some species, eyes are moved rapidly from side to side when an object moves within the visual field.

As mentioned, the shape of the head and the position of the eyes sacrifice binocular vision in snakes—the binocular field is only 30° to 40°—but the eyes' bulging positions on the sides of the head allow for excellent peripheral vision. Indeed, only a small field directly behind the snake is not visible. This is important for a predator, as the greater the visual field, the greater the chance of finding food and escaping harm from larger predators.

No matter how excellent their vision, snakes seem to respond mostly to movement. They may even act as if they are unaware of any object in their immediate vicinity that does not move. This

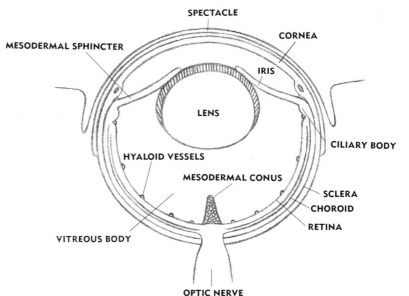

diagram of eye

must result from a brain that is designed to respond only to images that move across the retina, causing many retinal receptors to fire in series.

HEARING

The common wisdom is that snakes are deaf, so to avoid snakes when you walk through the woods you should stamp your feet and smash heavy sticks into the ground—the vibrations will be felt by the snakes and they will slither away. The truth is that many snakes do hear, and this sort of racket disturbs a lot of other animals.

We assume that because the snake lacks an external ear that it also lacks an internal ear. That is not so. Snakes have no external ears, no eardrums, no middle ears with the small bones or ossicles, and no Eustachian tubes connecting the middle ear with the pharynx. They do, however, have an inner ear with semicircular canals or bony labyrinths, a sacculus, and a utriculus—all structures used for balance and alignment of the head with gravity—and a cochlea, the bone containing the sound receptors. In a human or even a lizard ear, sound waves traveling through the air cause the eardrum to vibrate, which in turn causes the ossicles to vibrate. This vibration is transferred, via a small window in the cochlea, to the fluid within the cochlea. The vibrating fluid then stimulates sensory hairs on cells within a sensory organ, the organ of Corti, which rests on a basement membrane in the innermost recesses of the cochlea. In the snake, the quadrate bone, a small bone that connects the lower jaw to the top of the skull, may serve as a receptor for sound waves traveling through the air. The vibration of the quadrate and perhaps even the soft tissue around the cochlea, would, in turn, cause vibration of the fluid within the cochlea and, hence, stimulation of sound receptors.

Little work has been done on the snake ear and some recent books on reptiles ignore earlier work done on hearing in snakes by E. Wever and J. Vernon, who studied the ear in many species of reptiles. Wever and Vernon found that some species of colubrid snakes could hear quite well in the range of 0.1 to 0.7 kHz, with the best hearing in the range of 0.1 to 0.2 kHz. This is the range of very low-frequency, or deep, sounds. The hiss, a sound made as a threat by vertebrates from reptiles to primates, is an example of a low-frequency sound. Baby crocodiles hiss in the 0.1 to 0.4 kHz range. As snakes are not particularly vocal animals, but they do

hiss in threat displays, this means that snakes can hear the most important vocalization they make. This also would mean that they can hear hisses made by other animals. Vibrations picked up by the substrate via their lower jaws would also be transferred to the quadrate bone. So snakes in the woods can hear large animals, such as ourselves, coming, both through the airborne sound waves made by our footfalls and the vibrations transferred through the ground with each one of our steps.

SMELL: JACOBSON'S ORGAN AND CHEMORECEPTION

The snake's sense of smell is excellent. All amphibians and reptiles have a Jacobson's organ at some time in their lives. Jacobson's organ is a chemoreceptor (a sense organ that responds to chemicals) with cells specialized to fire in the presence of small amounts of chemicals. These chemicals are delivered to the organ via the snake's infamous forked tongue. It is impossible to discuss Jacobson's organ without discussing the tongue. Despite the idiom, "You speak with forked tongue," snakes do not use their bilobed tongues for speech. The tongue is a mechanism by which chemicals can be brought into contact with Jacobson's organ. Rapid flicking of the tongue, much more rapid than respirations, allows the snake to sample its environment. The anterior portion of the lips is slightly parted to allow the tongue to flick back and forth without the snake opening its mouth. Between flicks, the tongue nestles into the paired Jacobson's organs, where the stimulus is transmitted via chemical receptors directly to the olfactory bulbs within the brain, for interpretation of smell sensations.

If you watch a snake, you will see that it sticks out its tongue in different ways. This is because its tongue is much more efficient in sensing the environment if it is moved around. If alarmed, a rattlesnake poised to strike extends its tongue and holds it out with the fork spread wide for a long period of time to gather as much sensory information as possible before returning it to the mouth. During hunting, snakes flip their tongues in and out rapidly, frequently touching the ground as they travel. Snakes are very sensitive to smell and can follow scent trails. This sensitivity also makes captive snakes picky eaters. If the food it is offered does not smell right after being probed by its tongue, a snake will not eat.

THERMORECEPTORS

Pit vipers, boas, and most pythons are capable of detecting endothermic, or warm-blooded, animals through special infrared detectors they have on their faces. Pit vipers have loreal pits between the eye and nares or nostril, while pythons and boas have numerous infrared receptors on the upper or lower lip. The receptors detect differences in temperatures between objects within the environment and the background temperature. They are extremely sensitive—they can differentiate between objects that have as little as 0.5°F (0.2°C) difference between them.

In general, infrared receptors tend to be found on snakes that are noctural or at least hunt at night. These organs discriminate so well and so rapidly that it is not safe to be a mouse with a warm body roaming around at night in areas that are home to rattlesnakes.

It is thought that there are specific thermoreceptors within individual scales in some animals, although it also is possible that some of these pits are for sensing pain and touch.

All pit vipers, such as this Malabar pit viper, *Trimeresurus malabarensis*, have thermal receptors located on the side of the face between the eye and nostril. These heat-sensitive organs play an important role in the detection and capture of endothermic prey.

© Rom Whitaker

chapter four

HABITS AND BEHAVIOR

Surprisingly little is known about the complexities of snake behavior and what causes snakes to function as they do. We have yet to fully understand the workings of specialized sensory organs such as the pits that occur on the scales of the lips and face of some snakes; the way information finds its way from the tongue and Jacobson's organ to the brain and how it is interpreted; the processing of sound or vibration; or the physiological changes that take place as a result of varying environmental temperatures.

Snakes in the wild tend to be highly secretive. Even those that live above ground and are active during the day often take flight at the slightest disturbance. Therefore, scientists may have little opportunity for long-term observations. Few species are readily available for study under captive conditions, and then behavior patterns are frequently altered by environmental conditions that differ significantly from those in the animal's natural habitat. We know that different kinds of snakes, and even individuals, behave differently at night than they do during the day and behave one way at one temperature and quite differently at another. The yellow anaconda, *Eunectes notaeus*, is known for its nasty disposition in captivity. In the wild in Brazil, scientists walk up to them with impunity and pick them up behind their heads, because in the wild, the young bite, but for some reason, the adults do not. It is not unusual for someone donating a pet snake to a zoo to describe it as "a gentle animal that never bites," only to be surprised when the zookeeper handles the animal with cautious respect. A week later, the same animal often displays a defensive temperament that is more characteristic for the species because it is now maintained at an appropriately high temperature that is consistent with what the animal lives at in the wild. Information on the behavior of snakes kept under captive conditions may not represent naturalistic behavior due to inappropriate temperatures, insufficient food sources, inappropriate day-night cycles, and most importantly, the limitation of the size of the environment. The behaviors that are most likely to be observed in captivity are feeding, defensive, and reproductive behaviors.

HIBERNATION AND AESTIVATION

In the temperate regions of the world, winter cold periods often exceed the critical low temperature at which prolonged exposure will result in the death of the snake. This temperature is about 32° to 40°F (0° to 4°C). In cold weather, snakes and other reptiles seek protected sites and stay there until warm weather returns.

In the northeastern part of the United States, the timber rattlesnake, *Crotalus horridus*, lives in forested foothills and low mountain regions, where the eastern hemlock and the eastern white pine flourish. A primary characteristic of this habitat is the presence of rocky hillsides containing rock ledges, fissures, and slides, with a southeastern or southwestern exposure that is exposed to the low angles of the winter sun. The habitat is often shared with the northern copperhead, *Agkistrodon c. mokeson*; pilot black snake, *Elaphe obsoleta*; milk snake, *Lampropeltis triangulum*; eastern garter snake, *Thamnophis sirtalis*; black racer, *Coluber constrictor*; and an assortment of other small reptiles and amphibians.

Opposite: The timber rattlesnake, *Crotalus horridus*, of the eastern and central United States, hibernates in dens from late October to April. In the northern parts of its range, dens are found in rocky outcroppings on hills.

The cycle of hibernation begins as the days shorten and the nights grow cooler. In late August and early September, timber rattlesnakes return to the upper hillsides and rocky retreats that they have used year after year for hibernation during the long, cold winter. Females arrive first, heavy with young, and give birth. They begin to congregate near the entrance to selected underground chambers as the days continue to shorten. Finally, near the end of October, the snakes move into the chambers. They do not feed for several weeks prior to retreating, for it would not be desirable to have food in the stomach for so many months during which the digestive enzymes do not function due to the decreased temperature. Besides, food is unnecessary, as hibernating animals maintain minimal physiological activity. Hibernation chambers remain at temperatures between 40°F (4°C) and 52°F (11°C) throughout the year, from the deepest recesses to the chamber entrance. Once inside the chamber, breathing and metabolism slow down. Energy and moisture are conserved. Indeed, studies have shown that snakes emerging after months of hibernation have experienced little weight loss from their long fast at these low temperatures.

Winter snow covering the ground combines with the minimal warmth of the winter sun to maintain the hibernaculum chamber at temperatures above freezing. If the snakes have chosen a chamber unwisely—one that is not deep enough—or the snow is insufficient to cover the ground with an insulating blanket, the temperature of the chamber can drop to freezing and all of the snakes will die.

As the days begin to lengthen again, the snows melt and a gradual warming takes place. One of the mysteries of hibernation is that retreat and emergence are not tied to short-term cold or warm climatic conditions. For example, if spring temperatures rise prematurely, the snakes do not emerge from hibernation. Rather, their emergence is related to the lengthening of the day and the general warming of the entire habitat. Emergence rarely takes place before April 15, and generally the snakes are out of hibernation by May 2.

As soon as the snakes emerge they shed their skins and begin to feed. Breeding occurs very soon, and as spring ends, the snakes disperse to the lower elevations and fields.

When the snakes prepare to retreat for the winter and again when they are just emerging from hibernation, many animals may be encountered in a very small area at the same time, in the same place, year after year. Unscrupulous animal dealers take advantage of these periods and collect large numbers of snakes for sale to snake shows and private collectors. Entire populations of animals are easily decimated. Many of the captured snakes refuse to feed and die under poor captive conditions.

Climatic conditions opposite to those causing hibernation lead to aestivation. In some hot climates, during the time of year when temperatures rise extremely high and drought occurs, snakes and other reptiles and amphibians may burrow into mud or deep into soil banks where they are protected by the cooler temperatures. They preserve body moisture by coiling together in small chambers. Some snakes become encased in a ball of hardened mud, where they remain until the rains come again and they are liberated as the soil or mud softens.

The timber rattlesnake, *Crotalus horridus*, hibernates in dens in winter. As suitable dens may be few and far between, several species of snakes, venomous and non-venomous alike, may share winter quarters.

© P. Brazaitis

REPRODUCTIVE BEHAVIOR

In the wild, most snakes have regular breeding cycles that conform to environmental factors, although some tropical snakes may breed year round. Factors that may affect time of breeding include day length, average daily temperature, and rainfall or presence of a dry season. Interestingly, captive snakes also maintain specific breeding cycles very similar to those the species maintains in the wild. Thus, a well-versed zookeeper in New York will know that the Burmese python, *Python molurus bivittatus*, will lay eggs between December and February. The male and female should be put together for mating two months prior to the egg-laying date. If, for some reason, the breeding season is disrupted, a disproportionate number of malformed embryos or infertile ova may be produced.

Breeding generally occurs immediately after aestivation during prolonged hot, dry periods or hibernation during cold winter periods. Snakes from temperate regions often will not breed

SNAKE EGGS

Reptiles were the first land animals to produce an egg in which an embryo grew, enveloped in a protective, nourishing sac called an amnion. The amnion envelops the embryo in fluid, which prevents the embryo from drying out, while the yolk sac provides nourishment. As the embryo develops, it expels carbon dioxide, which escapes through minute pores in the leathery eggshell. Eggs that are too closely packed with soil can die from suffocation. The amount of moisture around the eggs is also impor-

tant. The shell may expand and swell when water is absorbed from outside the egg, or the egg may collapse and dent when there is insufficient water. Unlike bird eggs, once laid, snake eggs may not be rotated or the embryo can tear loose from the yolk sac and drown. As a result, snake eggs have an adhesive covering when laid that makes the eggs stick together in a stable mass.

Incubation temperatures are critical to the developing embryo. Temperatures that are too high

can result in deformities and accelerated growth. Temperatures that are too low can result in poor development and death. Snakes generally select a protected retreat for egg laying, and they very often choose an area where decaying organic material is especially plentiful and burrow temperatures and humidity remain stable and within the necessary incubation temperature range. For some species, termite mounds, alligators' nests, and old sawdust piles are favorite sites.

unless they have been subjected to a period of prolonged cooling. In captivity, snakes may have to be subjected to cooler temperatures for a period of time to induce breeding. Afterward, hormonal levels will rise and males will seek out females who are very receptive. Female snakes are usually larger than males.

Different species have different courtship patterns. Breeding often begins with the male approaching the female and rubbing his chin on her back. He then proceeds to make a series of slow jerking advances accompanied by rapid tongue flicking and may drape himself over the female's back and rapidly rub her tail with his as courtship continues. If she is receptive, she will eventually raise her tail and mating takes place. A single copulation may last for many hours. Males can use either one of their two hemipenes in copulation. The spines, spurs, convolutions, and folds of the hemipenis fit into receptors in the female's cloaca. In some species, females can store viable sperm for more than a year after insemination, finally developing offspring when suitable climatic conditions prevail.

After copulation, the male and female part company. Some species (called viviparous) bear living young, while others (called

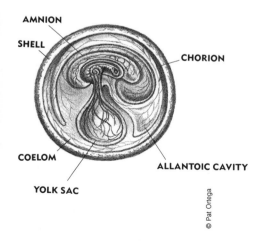

AMNION

SHELL

CHORION

COELOM

ALLANTOIC CAVITY

YOLK SAC

© Pat Ortega

Stages in the development of the night adder, *Causus rhombeatus*: embryo at 28 days (left) and 40 days (center).

© Rom Whitaker

These Asiatic cobras, *Naja naja*, have just hatched from their eggs. The snakelet's hood is spread wide in a display of irritation, and the snake is already capable of inflicting a venomous bite.

oviparous) lay eggs that are soft and leathery. Those species that are long and streamlined in body shape generally lay eggs that are elongated and cigar shaped while short, stout snakes lay eggs that are oval.

The eggs are laid in a location that will provide the proper environmental temperature and moisture for incubation. Incubation temperatures vary among species, but generally are between 84°F (29°C) and 90°F (32°C). Incubating eggs grow and gain weight. Most female snakes do not coil around their eggs during the average six- to nine-week incubation period, but some, like the king cobra, *Ophiophagus hannah*, build a nest of leaves into which they deposit their eggs and then coil around and guard the eggs during incubation. Some pythons coil around their eggs and constrict their coils, creating heat to aid in incubation.

The notorious bushmaster, *Lachesis muta*, of South and Central America, lies coiled around her eggs in a moist, cool retreat. Although she will remain to guard her eggs for nearly two months, she cannot raise her body temperature, as do some pythons, to warm the eggs.

© David T. Roberts

PYTHONS AND THEIR WAYS

They mate in the autumn. And their dormant season (winter-time) supervenes before another batch of eggs is produced in South Africa's mid-summer.

The number of eggs varies according to the size of the snake. Twenty-three is the smallest number produced by one of our captive pythons, sixty-nine the maximum. The following record provides some instances:

Python	feet in length	laid	eggs
Python 11	11¾	,,	23
,,	12½	,,	31
,,	13	,,	29
,,	13¾	,,	38
,,	14½	,,	44
,,	15	,,	54
,,	15	,,	51
,,	15¼	,,	62
,,	16	,,	58
,,	17	,,	57
			69

The eggs vary from five to five and a half ounces in weight; the shells are soft, tough, leathery, and in colour ivory white. There is no distinct yolk and transparent albumen as in the eggs of birds; the whole is of a yellow tint.

In some species the eggs, when laid, are in the early stage of incubation—the very young,

14

A PYTHON AND HER EGGS

After producing her eggs the mother python coiled her body round them in the form of a cone, with her head resting on top, so that the eggs were invisible. When we approached she partly uncoiled and remained on the defensive.

pulsating embryo being plainly visible when the egg is opened. The African Python's eggs are usually, but not always, quite fresh when produced.

Out in the wild, pythons deposit their eggs in a variety of places. The deserted hole of an ant-eater, or aard-vark, is a favourite nest. So is any other kind of hole or cavity in the rocks sufficiently large, or the hollow trunk of a tree. Other favoured egg-nests are the cavities among the roots of large trees growing out of a tangled mass of undergrowth ; among dead leaves amid dense scrub ; under tufts of long, rank grass ; in sugar-cane plantations ; in the midst of rushes bordering streams.

Our captive pythons have often laid great batches of eggs, mostly during December and January, though we had one instance of a python laying a pile of fully developed eggs in October, and another of a similar delivery in November.

In the wild state the mother snake lies coiled round her eggs for the twofold purpose of protecting them from the many enemies—or other creatures of the wild—who would eat them, and of aiding them in the process of incubation. At

this period her blood rises to a temperature of 90° Fahrenheit, which is, apparently, Nature's rule for the hatching of infant pythons.

Among our captives the parent sometimes remains coiled round the eggs for several days after laying them ; but we have never noticed any keen desire on her part to protect or continue to incubate them. This may be due to the strange environment, and to the nervousness and shyness contingent upon captivity.

On one occasion a python threw her coils around her pile of eggs and remained thus, immovable, until disturbed by some of her fellow-captives in the cage. Thereupon she uncoiled herself, moved away, and took no further notice of her eggs.

When the young ones hatch out the mother shows that she considers her maternal duties at an end by taking no heed of them. The babes scatter in all directions in the instinctive desire for food—at this period consisting of such small prey as mice, rats, birds, lizards, and frogs. They would probably hatch out equally well if the mother did not coil about them, as other young reptiles do. But the python knows that if she does not guard her eggs very few will survive,

16

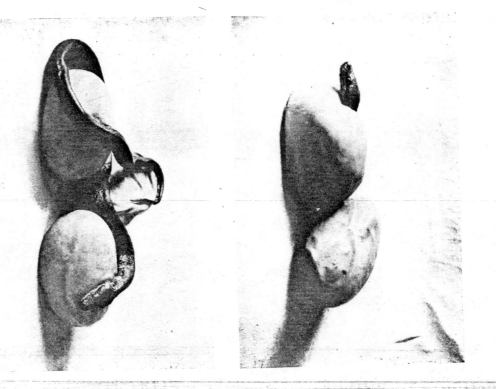

1. A Baby Python's First Glimpse of Terrestrial Life
2. Resting after a Hard Struggle to get out of the Shell

16

so many are the creatures on the look-out for these titbits. Chief among these enemies are the large monitor lizard, the mongoose, the jackal, and the rat.

A pair of African Pythons once mated in the London Zoo in the month of June. The female laid close upon a hundred eggs in the following January, and incubated them until April, when the embryos were found to be still immature. This retarded incubation was undoubtedly due to the unnatural conditions, for the eggs should not have taken longer than between two and three months to hatch.

The following account of a python incubating her eggs is taken from Harmsworth's *Natural History* :

It had long been reported in India that pythons incubated their large spherical eggs—which may be compared in size to lawn-tennis balls. Such reports were received incredulously until their truth was established in 1841, when a female African python, in the Jardin des Plantes, Paris, laid fifteen eggs on 6th May, and proceeded to incubate them. When first laid, the eggs, which were completely separate, were soft, oval, and ashy-grey ; they soon assumed a rounder form and clearer tint, at the same time hardening. The parent collected them into a cone-shaped pile, and coiled herself round it in such a way

© Bruce Foster

The reticulated python, *Python reticulatus*, coils around her 40 to 60 eggs to protect them and conserve moisture. The species does not have the ability to increase its body temperature through muscle contractions during the incubation period, as is typical for the Burmese python.

A few pythons, including the Burmese python, Python m. bivittatus, *of Southeast Asia, not only coil around their eggs during incubation but can regulate their body temperatures to some degree during the process. Researchers at the New York Zoological Park found that incubating Burmese pythons could actually raise and lower their body temperatures several degrees by rapidly contracting their muscles in what is often described as a "hiccup." The entire body lurches with each contraction. The snake needs to maintain a temperature of about 90°F (32°C) for the eggs to hatch. To do so, she coils tightly around the eggs, completely enveloping them in her coils. Her head is at the top, and she remains with her snout tucked down in the coils with her chin on the eggs. Burmese pythons have heat receptors on the front scales of their lips, and it is presumed the female monitors her egg temperatures with those receptors. Should the temperature and surrounding air temperature drop, she will coil more tightly around the eggs and the rate of her muscular contractions will increase to generate more heat. A rise in the environmental temperature will lower the rate of her contractions and she will open her coils to allow the eggs to cool. During the entire two- to three-month incubation period, the female Burmese python will not feed. In the early stages, she will drink water only if it comes within reach as she sits on the eggs. Later during the incubation period, she will leave the eggs only for short periods of time and will return immediately after drinking and bathing.*

*L*ike all snakes, baby bull snakes, *Pituophis Melanoleucus,* have a small sharp projection on the tip of the snout called an "egg tooth." As the time for hatching arrives, the youngsters use the egg tooth to break the egg and make a hole through which they can emerge. Baby snakes often remain with their heads sticking out of the eggs for a day or two before leaving the eggs. The egg tooth is lost a few days later. Once the eggs hatch, the mother has no further interest in her young.

© Johan Marais

Vipers and boas give birth to living young. After a gestation period of three to six months, the female gives birth to completely developed baby snakes. Each is expelled from the cloaca of the female in a transparent membranous sac or "egg" from which it quickly breaks out. In some species, the offspring break out of their membranous sac before the female expels them. No matter how the young are born, the total period between conception and hatching or birth is about the same for most snake species.

FEEDING

Whether born alive or hatched from an egg, the period of "birth" generally coincides with a time when there is an abundance of food for the young snakes to eat immediately. Food items for snakes include small frogs or tadpoles, specific insects or larvae,

small mice, birds, and other reptiles. Some baby snakes, like the copperhead, *Agkistrodon contortrix*, have a bright yellow tail that is distinct from the body. The tip of the tail has a tiny black spot on each side that gives the tail the appearance of an insect grub or caterpillar. The baby snake, which is banded in browns and reds, is inconspicuous in dry forest leaves except for the tail. Waving slowly in an upright position, the tail appears to be a tasty insect to the small frogs that make up part of the baby snake's diet. Many baby snakes use similar lure techniques quite effectively to procure food.

Copperheads, *Agkistrodon contortrix*, are one of the many species of snakes whose offspring have brightly colored tails, which they wave slowly to act as a lure to attract prey. The color is lost as the snakes reach maturity and change food preferences.

 ## MATERNAL BEHAVIOR

*M*ost snakes show no maternal care for their young; however, the common anaconda, *Eunectes murinus, is a snake that gives birth to young that are born in a membranous sac or emerge from the sac while still* inside the female's body just prior to birth. When the babies are born, the female methodically seizes each one in her jaws and allows it to crawl through her many sharp needle-like teeth to clean it and remove the placenta that attached it to the egg membranes. The babies are not injured in the process. Stillborn young and discarded membranes are eaten by the female. When all trace of the birth is gone, maternal care ends.

The Natal green snake, *Philothamnus natalensis*, of South Africa, eating a gecko lizard.

Snakes are well adapted for the different types of food they consume. Each species has its own food preferences. Snakes catch their prey by one of three methods: overpowering, constriction, or envenomation (injection of venom). We generally think of snakes as feeding on warm-blooded prey such as mice, rats, or a variety of small mammals and birds. For some species, food items also include frogs and other amphibians in any developmental stage; fish, lizards, and other snakes; insects, crustaceans, and a multitude of other invertebrates. Some species race after their prey, which tends to be small in size, overpower it by catching it with their jaws, and then swallow it alive; others stalk prey slowly, seize it with their jaws in a quick strike, and quickly coil around the prey's rib cage using their strong constricting muscles to prevent the prey from breathing. Few animals can escape the grasp and coils of a large constrictor. Giant snakes such as the reticulated python, *Python reticulatus*, may, on occasion, eat small goats, calves, and pigs, while the preferred meal of the yellow anaconda, *Eunectes notaeus*, is the South American caiman, a crocodilian related to the American alligator. These twenty-five-foot(7.6-m)-long monster snakes have also been known to swallow a small human.

Let's take a look at some of the highly specialized species and their prey.

The king cobra, *Ophiophagus hannah*, feeds entirely on other snakes, killing its prey with a large quantity of highly neurotoxic venom. It is immune to the effects of the venom of most elapid

Rodents comprise the diet of a great many snakes around the world. The African house snake, *Lamprophis fuliginosus*, often provides its services in and around homes and gardens.

A desert kingsnake, above, *Lampro-peltis getulus holbrooki*, constricts a snake. Kingsnakes appear to have some degree of immunity to snake venoms and include venomous species in their diets.

snakes and attacks kraits, *Bungarus* species, and other cobras with impunity. However, in captivity, when confronted by a snake with a large head shape that suggests it is a viper, family Viperidae, the attack is quite different. Viper venom differs from that of the king cobra and the king cobra is not immune to it. Vipers also have long fangs that might inflict injury. In this situation, the cobra approaches slowly, arching its body and head high over the viper. Striking downward, the cobra seizes the snake immediately behind its head and holds on until the snake is dead before swallowing it.

The snail-eating snake of South America, *Dipsas variegata*, has a modified extended lower jaw that allows it to reach into the shells of snails and extricate them.

There are many constricting snake-eating species such as king snakes, *Lampropeltis*, file snakes, *Mehelya*, and the mussuranas of the genus *Clelia* that prefer to kill and eat the large venomous South American pit vipers.

Members of the African genus *Aparallactus* feed exclusively on scorpions and centipedes, while the yellow-lipped sea snake of Fiji feeds entirely on small eels. Large North American water snakes, *Nerodia*, have been found with the pectoral and dorsal spines of large catfish, which the snake had swallowed, protruding through the snake's body wall. A wild-caught seventeen-foot (5-m) common anaconda, *Eunectes murinus*, that arrived at the New York Zoological Park had difficulty feeding until it defecated the dorsal and terminal back plates from the shell of a sixty-pound (27-kg) yellow-footed tortoise it had consumed prior to capture. Others, like the small North American brown snake, *Storeria dekayi*, have difficulty overcoming a large earthworm.

An arboreal carpet python, opposite, *Morelia spilotes*, hangs upside down to let gravity help it swallow a bird. Most of Australia's pythons are long and slender and feed on lizards as well.

Many of the bones that comprise a snake's skull, particularly the jaws, are held together by elastic ligaments and muscles. The lower jaw is not fused together as it is in mammals, so the jaw has great flexibility. Indeed, each side of the snake's mandible can stretch away from and separate from the other. Snakes also lack breast- and collarbones; these would encase the body cavity and restrict its internal diameter. The snake's skin is capable of extreme expansion, like so much elastic cloth.

Once the snake catches and kills its prey, such as a rat or mouse, the snake examines it closely for any signs of life by prodding it with its snout and flicking its tongue. Any movement and the snake will begin the process of killing the prey again. When it is sure that the prey is dead and rendered harmless, the snake searches for the head of the animal and begins to eat it. Seizing the rodent by the tip of the snout, the snake uses one row of teeth after another to draw the prey into its throat. The snake has over 200 pointed, recurved teeth in two rows on the bottom jaw and four rows on the top jaws. Each row of teeth moves independently of the other. As the snake draws more of its meal into its throat, the jaws and skin

stretch. Snakes have a breathing tube called the epiglottis behind the sheathed tongue on the lower jaw. When large prey is filling the mouth, the epiglottis opens to allow the snake to breathe freely. Eventually the snake gets its mouth past the widest part of the prey, usually the shoulders, then the pelvis, until the prey is fully inside the expanded neck. The snake then constricts its neck and body muscles rhythmically and literally forces the rodent down into its stomach.

Depending on the snake's body temperature and metabolism, food usually takes about a week to ten days to fully digest. During that time, the snake remains quiet and in retreat. Highly active snakes, such as racers, need to feed nearly daily, while less active varieties, such as the stout Gaboon viper, *Vipera gabonica,* may feed barely once every several weeks and may defecate once or twice every two to three months.

It is thought that the venom injected by some snakes into their prey is a necessary digestive aid in that it actually begins the process of breaking down the prey's tissue even before it is ingested by the snake. In this way, the venom has a second, valuable use because it helps the snake digest its prey more quickly.

© John Visser

A venomous twig snake's, *Thelotornis kirtlandii*, slender, speckled body blends with the surrounding foliage. Like other, similar snakes, it may sway slowly to imitate a vine in the wind.

DEFENSES

Snakes use a number of ways to defend themselves. These include aggression toward intruders in the form of attack or bluff behavior, flight to escape, displays to threaten and frighten, camouflage, feigning death, expression of musk or feces, or simple defensive retaliation when attacked or seized.

The majority of snakes immediately attempt to escape by fleeing at the slightest annoyance. This is true of venomous as well as nonvenomous species, particularly the water snakes, racers, whipsnakes, and most of the cobras. Some snakes will stand their ground, ready to respond if an attack takes place, but will not attack the attacker. These species include rattlesnakes, vipers, and some cobras.

A very few species are notorious for their furious attacks upon intruders, particularly during the breeding season. The king cobra, *Ophiophagus hannah*, which grows to lengths of up to 18.5 feet (5.6 m) is one such species. Even in captivity, king cobras are highly dangerous animals that are not to be trifled with. Once aroused, a king cobra will rear the anterior third of its body off the ground and, standing with its neck flattened in a long tapering hood, will squarely face the intruder. If the intruder dares to move closer, arousal turns to serious threat.

The king cobra, with head up and hood expanded, prepares to defend itself and may attack.

Mouth open, emitting a deep short hiss, the snake attacks. First rushing forward with its whole body, the snake attempts to deliver a bite at the end of the rush with a great downward strike. A bite is accompanied by momentary chewing to ensure that a large quantity of highly toxic venom is injected. If the first attempt fails, the snake will rush and strike again. A large king cobra can cover ten feet (3 m) or more with each attack. Elephants have been known to die from envenomation when bitten on the highly vascularized trunk by a king cobra.

Another highly dangerous species is the black mamba of Africa, *Dendroaspis polylepis*. Black mambas often exceed ten feet (3 m) in length, maintain a high body temperature and activity level, and are nervous. The black mamba's fangs are among the longest found in an elapid and are set close to the front of its mouth. Some attacks are said to be virtually unprovoked, but in reality, they take place when an unaware intruder comes within a few yards of the snake without realizing it is there. This often occurs during the breeding season, when large males tend to be warmed by the sun, excited, and territorial. The snake rushes toward the offender with its mouth open to expose the black inside coloration. Often the snake is so large that a bite on the trunk of a person's body or as high up as the face and neck is not unusual. The snake may inflict several bites almost simultaneously in a frenzy of erratic behavior. Stories exist of several people and their horses being killed by a single surprised snake.

Such tales are probably exaggerated, but not impossible.

When annoyed, most snakes will vibrate their tails rapidly, sometimes open their mouths threateningly, and may suddenly expel air in a loud hiss. Much of this behavior is designed to intimidate a would-be attacker. In some species, it is accompanied by other displays. Asiatic cobras, *Naja naja*, are all too familiar in their formidable defensive posture of standing erect with the neck flattened into a hood. Each race or subspecies has a different pattern on the back of the hood and, in many instances, a different hood shape. However, herpetologists who work with Asiatic cobras know from experience that the species is very reluctant to bite, and even when it does, it fails to inject venom in more than half of the bites. At the first provocation, the snake rears the front third of its body and spreads its hood, facing the intruder. Should the disturbance continue, the cobra might make several quick strikes. Sometimes these, too, are bluffs and the strike is made with the mouth closed. If these actions do not succeed in repelling the attacker, the snake may turn around and display the back of the hood and markings to the source of the threat. The hood is designed to give the impression that the snake's head is bigger than it really is and that the snake should be left alone. If all else fails, the cobra will make every attempt to escape or may even feign death. Nonetheless, when truly aroused, cobras are dangerous animals indeed. They bite and chew, inflicting a serious bite that often results in the death of the victim.

Black mambas, *Dendroaspis polylepis*, are among the world's most dangerous snakes. Aggressive by nature, the snake's venom is extremely potent and bites are often fatal.

Some of the African spitting cobras go a step further. Their fangs are modified to direct venom outward and frontward rather than downward. The rinkhals, *Hemachatus haemachatus*, a cobra of the open veldt, also rears the front of its body and spreads a hood when disturbed. If the intruder appears to be persistent, the snake will suddenly seem to draw back its upper lips and strike forward with a short, loud hiss. In the process, a great spray of venom emerges from its fangs, like a shotgun blast, and flies toward the face of the intruder. If the victim is struck in the eyes, there is immediate intense pain followed by temporary blindness. Permanent visual impairment can result. Should the intruder seize the snake, the snake will roll over, open its mouth, and play dead. Foolhardy people have handled "dead" rinkhals with impunity, but to do so is to invite a very dangerous bite. The black-necked spitting cobra, *Naja nigricollis*, behaves much as the rinkhals but differs in that the venom, in large quantities, is "spit" in a solid stream and directed specifically at the eyes of an intruder. The snake is accurate up to eight or nine feet (2.5–2.7 m). The harmless hognose snake, *Heterodon platyrhinos*, of the United States also strikes, hisses, and then rolls over, feigning death with its mouth open and tongue hanging out when threatened. However, this species almost never bites, even if you put your finger in its mouth!

The twig snake, *Thelotornis kirtlandii*, inflates only the neck behind the head to display the contrasting white skin between the scales, negating its protective coloration. The red tongue is often held straight out in threat.

© Johan Marais

Some snakes, harmless and venomous alike, use various neck and body displays to intimidate an attacker. The boomslang, *Dispholidus typus*, and South American tiger rat snake, *Spilotes pullatus*, inflate and gyrate the entire neck area down through the body. The twig snake, *Thelotornis capensis*, of Africa inflates the region of the throat in a ball tapering down the neck. Water snakes, *Nerodia*, flatten the head and body, thrash their tails, and spray musk and feces in a threatening, but harmless display. On the other hand, there is no mistaking the deadly serious intentions of a tropical rattlesnake, *Crotalus durissus*, as it draws its body into a springlike coil, rattling furiously, with the front half of its body held high and quivering in a striking position as the snake judges the distance to the attacker or prey.

The timber rattlesnake, *Crotalus horridus*, is poised to strike with its head in an S curve. The snake can strike the entire length of the curve.

Many species depend on blending with their surroundings for defense or, if that fails, quickly racing to escape. The harmless green snakes of the United States, *Ophiodrys*, and the deadly green mamba, *Dendroaspis angusticeps*, are rarely seen except as escaping green blurs.

Other harmless species have evolved to look and behave like venomous species. The nonvenomous Southeast Asian red-tailed rat snake, *Gonyosoma oxycephala*, has a green body and a red tail, lives in green plants, and is quick to bite. A number of species of venomous green pit vipers with red tails occupy the same habitat, often in the same regions. The brightly banded false coral snakes, *Oxyrhopus*, of the Americas are well known to live and behave like their venomous coral snake, *Micrurus*, counterparts. Numerous snakes utilize protective coloration as a first line of defense and as an advantage in securing food. The northern copperhead, *Agkistrodon contortrix mokeson*, is virtually invisible as it sits on a bed of dry dead leaves. Many snakes are stepped on, walked by, or nearly sat upon and never move to reveal themselves. The Gaboon viper, *Bitis gabonica*, reaches lengths of six feet (2 m) or more and may be eight inches (20 cm) in diameter, yet place the brown, gray, and tan body in a small bed of dried jungle leaves and it disappears from view.

Every species has its own interesting and unique adaptations for survival. We need only to look to find them.

A neotropical green palm viper, *Bothrops nigroviridis*, lies concealed and motionless, covered with dew.

The California mountain king-snake, left, *Lampropeltis zonata*, is one of the North American mimics of the coral snake.

Below: Protective coloration may include dark patterns on a nondescript body color. This diamondback water snake, *Nerodia rhombifera*, is hidden amid the twigs and grasses.

© R. Andrew Odum

HABITATS AND POPULATIONS

*S*nakes are ectotherms—meaning that their body temperatures are controlled by the external environment. They therefore must live in regions that are warm for enough of the year to allow them time for active feeding, growth, and reproduction. The average snake is active at temperatures near 88°F (30°C). Some species begin activity at lower temperatures and others at higher temperatures, but in general, the optimal temperature range for snake activity is from 69.8°F to 98.6°F (21°C to 37°C). Snakes maintain their body temperatures by basking in the sun, coiling, burrowing underground (where it tends to be warmer than on the surface), and in some species, by coiling together in larger aggregations. The method used depends on the species of snake and on its habitat. For example, the yellow-bellied sea snake, *Pelamis platurus*, has a darkly pigmented back that absorbs the warm rays from the sun as the snake swims along near the surface of the ocean. This maintains the snake's body temperature at several degrees above the water's temperature. By moving downward in the water, the snake can cool itself or prevent further heating. It is well known that while incubating egg masses, pythons increase their body heat by muscular constrictions. It is not, however, known if the python uses the same technique to warm itself when it is not incubating eggs.

A snake must maintain its optimal body temperature in order for the enzyme systems that keep it alive to stay active. For example, if a snake is subjected to a low temperature immediately after eating a meal, it will not be able to digest the food. The digestive enzymes that break down the food will be inactive. As a result, the snake may die from effects of bacterial action on the food remaining within its stomach, including bloating caused by putrefaction of the undigested meal. Cold temperatures are also known to have a damaging if not lethal effect on developing embryos. Therefore, reproduction must occur during a time of year when eggs will not cool or freeze and newborn or newly hatched young will be able to find food. Thus, it is vital that snakes live in environments warm enough to support their habits and physiology.

Sea snakes bask at the surface of the water to thermoregulate and dive to cool. The yellow-bellied sea snake, *Pelamis platurus*, is found only in the tropical waters of the Indo-Pacific Oceans. It remains at sea even while giving birth to live young.

If you look at the worldwide distribution of snake species you will find that no snakes exist in areas where there is permafrost, that is, where the subsoil is frozen year round. There are some northerly species, however. The common adder of Europe reaches to the Arctic Circle in Scandinavia. The common garter snake of North America, *Thamnophis sirtalis*, is even found in Alaska. In the Southern Hemisphere, the most southerly occurring snake is the crotaline, *Bothrops ammodytoides*, which ranges from the warm Brazilian forests to Santa Cruz, Argentina. Snakes are also limited in their abilities to survive in the colder high altitudes. The Himalayan pit viper, *Agkistrodon himalayanus*, lives in elevations up to 16,400 feet (5,000 meters) above sea level, but it is the only snake that can survive in these conditions in the wild.

If you were to look at the distribution of snake species throughout the world, you would find that the areas with the most abundant species of snakes are in the tropics, with fewer and fewer species as you worked your way north and south into the temperate zones. You would also find fewer species at the highest elevations and more species at the lower elevations. Sea snakes, which live in the oceans, are very unusual. There are no

The garter snake, *Thamnophis sirtalis*, hibernates in winter. It is very cold-tolerant and is often the first snake species to emerge in the spring and one of the last to retreat in the fall.

© John Visser

The African egg-eating snake, *Dasypeltis inornata*, need not compete with other snakes for mice, birds, and lizards. By eating birds' eggs, it preys on a continuously available natural resource.

sea snakes in the Atlantic Ocean. They are found only in the Pacific and Indian Oceans. Although many theories abound as to why the sea snakes are limited in their range, including theories about their possible recent evolution, lack of an ecological niche in Atlantic waters, and temperature and currents of Pacific waters, no theory satisfactorily explains their distribution.

Some scientists ascribe differences in snake population distributions to amounts of habitat available. In other words, they believe that one area may have five species and another similar area only two species because the area with five species has more available snake habitat. Others attribute the differences to the amount of food available. An area with more food would have more snakes than an area with less food. In truth, there are many factors that work to determine how densely an area is populated with snakes and how many species of snakes are present in the area. Different species sharing the same habitat may be able to partition the habitat according to factors such as types of plants present, amount of moisture, soil types, and so on. They also may be able to diversify their food preferences so that they do not both prey on the same species. We tend to think of snakes as rodent eaters (probably as a result of the numerous televised wildlife movies showing a snake eating a mouse or rat), but different species are highly specialized in their dietary habits. Some of the small burrowing colubrids in the United States, such as the worm snakes, *Carphophis amoenus*, ringneck snakes, *Diadophis punctatus*, and rough earth snakes, *Virginia striatula*, eat earthworms. Some burrowing typhlopids feed on ants and termites. Eastern and southern hognose snakes eat frogs and toads. The aquatic striped swamp snake, *Regina alleni*, mainly lives on crayfish, although it also eats frogs and dwarf sirens, highly aquatic salamanders. Young snakes, which are smaller than adults and cannot ingest the large prey items adults can eat, may have different dietary requirements due to their rapid growth and higher energy needs. Young *Regina*, for example, prey upon dragonfly nymphs and some shrimp and crayfish. Researchers have shown that the quantity and quality of energy available to young *Regina* from their diet is greater than that provided by the adult diet.

Not only do individuals of the same species occupy different niches in the food chain at different times of their lives, but animals who eat similar foods, such as mammal-eating snakes,

The ringneck snake, *Diadophis punctatus*, of the eastern United States, feeds largely on salamanders, slugs, and earthworms.

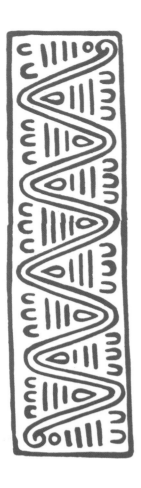

will, when sharing the same habitat, specialize in eating different prey. In habitats containing many snake species, the snakes have been found to specialize on food supplies at different trophic levels: some eat mammals, others eat birds, others eat reptiles, some eat different species of frogs, and still others eat eggs. There may be little or no overlap in the diets among the various snake species.

If you wished to determine the most numerous snakes in any habitat, you would have a very hard time. To begin with, snakes are fairly secretive creatures. Also, in temperate regions, it must be the correct season to find active snakes. During autumn, winter, and early spring, snakes may be hibernating in their burrows or caves. Unless you know exactly where they stay during hibernation, you may decide that there are no snakes present. Even during the warmer seasons, the day must be warm enough for the snake to be out basking, but not so hot that the snake is hiding in a cooler spot. If you are lucky, you may find a snake up and around during mating season, but in temperate regions, most snakes only mate once a year. Also, the snake's circadian or daily rhythm determines when or whether you will see it. A nocturnal species such as the cottonmouth moccasin, *Agkistrodon piscivorus*, is not likely to be up and about in the early morning, although many may be seen basking in the late afternoon.

Counting tropical species is equally difficult. On very hot days, the animals may aestivate, resting inactive in a cooler shaded area. And even at the best of times, most snakes are well camouflaged in their environment by their coloration. Therefore, estimates of numbers of snakes per species in any given habitat are apt to be incorrect. Even so, some intrepid biologists have tried to count some temperate zone species. What they found was that the smallest snakes, especially those that burrow, are more densely packed per acre than larger species. This in itself is not a great revelation, as small snakes tend to feed on highly abundant invertebrates, while large snakes tend to feed on much sparser populations of mammals, birds, frogs, or even other snakes.

Scientists know that disturbing the snake's habitat—through deforestation for agriculture, building roads, flooding, or developing it in other ways—affects the snakes and their populations. Unfortunately, in most cases we do not know enough about the populations and ecology of the snakes to know exactly how populations will be affected by these changes. Newer techniques, such as radio tracking using tiny computer chips and transmitters embedded into the snake's skin, and computerized modeling of habitats, may well aid in the study and elucidation of the life habits of snakes of all species.

The eastern cottonmouth water moccasin, *Agkistrodon piscivorus*, like other members of the genus around the world, feeds largely on fish and frogs.

chapter six

VENOMOUS SNAKES AND SNAKEBITES

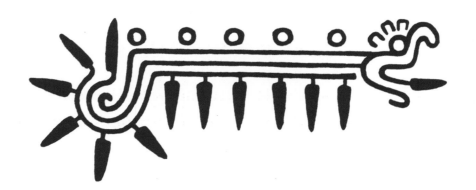

Differences between venomous and nonvenomous snakes may, at first glance, appear to be clear cut. Even in our society we educate young children about the danger of the fearsome cobra and rattlesnake, although it is only the latter that we are remotely likely to encounter on walks in parks and natural preserves. Car bumpers and even toys sport decals with drawings of these venomous snakes with their mouths gaping, oversized fangs poised for the bite. But there are many rear-fanged members of the colubroids, the most evolutionarily recent of all snake groups. Although the elapids, which include the cobras, and the viperids, which include rattlesnakes, are also members of the superfamily Colubroidea, the rear-fanged colubroids are members of the family Colubridae and are more closely related to the viperids.

Colubrids are the snakes we are most likely to see when we go out for walks in the woods,

swamps, or deserts. Garter snakes, kingsnakes, milk snakes, water snakes, racers—all are members of the colubrid family. Some people keep them at home as pets; children handle them at school or at visits to the zoos. What makes these snakes so safe to handle? The ancestors of these modern-day colubrids were venomous. At some point in evolution, some of them lost their venom glands and in others the venom glands were greatly reduced in size. A few even lost their rear fangs. Of those colubrids that maintain venom glands, some are extremely dangerous and have venom that is life threatening to humans, such as the African boomslang, *Dispholidus typus*. Others, such as the hognose snake, *Heterodon*, although not really considered a venomous species, have venom that may result in localized pain and swelling in the area of the bite, but in general, these snakes cannot even be forced to bite a person. Even when some of the rear-fanged colubrids do bite, envenomation does not necessarily occur. The fangs are so far back on the maxillary bone that in order to effect envenomation the snake must chew the bitten part to position it under the fangs. We don't often give the snakes a chance to do that.

Why do snakes have venom? Let us start by correcting a frequent misnomer. People often refer to "poisonous" snakes, and indeed, by dictionary definition, this is not incorrect. But herpetologists are sticklers for precision, and precisely, a poisonous snake, like a poisonous frog, would make you sick if you ingested it. There are no snakes that make you sick when you eat them. In fact, snake meat is considered to be quite delicious. Venom, on the other hand, enters the body of the victim by means other than ingestion—in the case of snakes, through injection from the fangs. The glands that produce the venom are called venom glands. And thus, we have the term, *venomous snakes*. The effects of venom may be neurotoxic—destroying or paralyzing the nervous system; cytotoxic—causing cellular destruction in the area of the bite; cardiotoxic—destroying or paralyzing heart tissue; or hemotoxic—destroying the blood-clotting mechanism. These different effects are collectively referred to as snake venom poisoning. The main function of venom is to immobilize or kill the snake's prey prior to ingestion and to begin the digestion of the prey with many digestive enzymes.

If the venom is so toxic, why doesn't the snake get sick? Why aren't there any poisoned venomous snakes? A snake is immune to both poisoning and envenomation from its own venom and can safely ingest its own venom and venom from related species with no ill effects. After all, the snake ingests its own venom along with its prey. A bite received from an unrelated species of venomous snake, however, is likely to be fatal. Thus, the king cobra, *Ophiophagus hannah*, which as its name implies, eats snakes (*ophio* refers to snakes, *phagos* means to eat), eats other

© John Visser

elapids with impunity, but must take special care that it is not bitten when it grabs a viperid such as Russell's viper, *Vipera russelli*.

Snakes also use their venom for defense. A venomous snake can defend itself from its enemies by biting them. Biting people in particular, causing them pain, tissue damage, and even death is not in itself a unique function of venom. After all, venomous snakes and, before them, venomous lizards evolved many millions of years before humans. People just happen to be unfortunate victims of the snake's behavior patterns.

Enlarged rear fang of a boomslang, *Dispholidus typus*. Unlike viper and elapid fangs, these fangs have a groove on one side along which the venom flows to saturate the wound the snake inflicts.

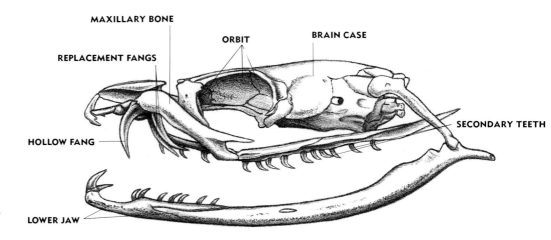

MAXILLARY BONE

ORBIT

BRAIN CASE

REPLACEMENT FANGS

HOLLOW FANG

SECONDARY TEETH

LOWER JAW

SKULL OF AN ELAPID SNAKE. THE FANGS ARE PERMANENTLY ERECT AND DO NOT FOLD BACK WHEN NOT IN USE.

There are three major groups of venomous snakes: the elapids, the viperids, and the rear-fanged colubrids. A fourth group, the family Atractaspidae, may be a primitive group of venomous snakes, present in Africa and the Middle East. All the venomous snakes are classified in the superfamily Colubroidea, the most evolutionarily recent of the snakes.

The elapids include the cobras, kraits, sea snakes, mambas, and coral snakes. Elapids are found in tropical and temperate regions throughout the world, excluding Europe. Their venom is produced by epithelial tissue, which is present in all glands, but in these snakes is specialized to produce venom. This gland is similar in both structure and function to venom glands seen in lizards. The fangs, located at the front of the jaw and in front of the eyes, are attached to the maxillary bone. The fangs have a fully enclosed groove and function like a hypodermic needle. At the time of the strike, a muscle that surrounds the venom gland contracts. This puts pressure on the venom gland and pushes the venom through the mucous membrane and venom duct at the base of the fang, then through the groove in the fang and into the victim.

It is thought that the elapids evolved from an ancestral form similar to the rear-fanged colubrids and that the fangs subsequently moved forward in the mouth, replacing the teeth at the front. The grooves, which were open in the more primitive snakes, closed, leaving the present-day enclosed groove, although some elapids, such as the sea snakes, still have open grooves in their fangs. Rear teeth remain in most of the elapids, although mambas have only fangs on their upper jaws. Some of the more primitive elapids, besides having fangs, may have rear teeth with open fanglike grooves. Elapid fangs are fixed in position in the front of the jaw and cannot be rotated or moved. They rest in a groove in the lower lip.

Viperids, which include the true vipers of the Old World and the pit vipers of the Old and New Worlds, have only fangs on the maxillary bone at the front of the jaw. Additional teeth are located on the pterygoid bone behind the maxillary. The maxillary bone is movable and can rotate upward and outward, causing the fangs, which are usually folded back on the roof of the mouth, to move forward when the snake is poised to strike. This arrangement of the fangs allows the fangs to be very long in some cases, thus providing the viperids with a more efficient venom delivery system than is seen in elapids and allowing the snake to attack larger prey with less effort. The fangs are hollow and ungrooved. Because of the toxicity of their venom, elapids are usually considered the world's most dangerous snakes to humans. However, some people consider viperids more dangerous because many species have toxic venom. Combined with the greater mobility and size of the fangs, this makes envenomation much easier.

Pit vipers, especially, are noted for the massive size of their heads. Some pit vipers need large head glands because they produce large quantities of relatively weak venom, while the Gaboon viper of Africa, *Bitis gabonica*, is particularly dangerous because the enormous glands produce large quantities of very toxic venom. A large head is needed to accommodate all of this extra equipment.

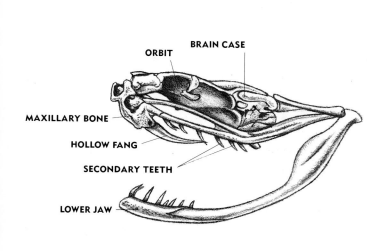

A VIPERID SKULL SHOWING THE ENLARGED, HOLLOW FANG FOLDED BACK AGAINST THE ROOF OF THE MOUTH.

BRAIN CASE

ORBIT

MAXILLARY BONE

HOLLOW FANG

SECONDARY TEETH

LOWER JAW

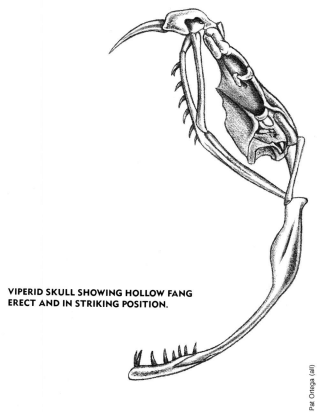

VIPERID SKULL SHOWING HOLLOW FANG ERECT AND IN STRIKING POSITION.

© Pat Ortega (all)

Most colubrids have lost the rear fangs, but those that retain rear fangs have grooved fangs at the rear of the jaw attached to Duvernoy's gland, the venom gland. Of these rear-fanged colubrids, only two are considered a potential threat to humans: the boomslang, *Dispholidus typus*, and the African twig snake, *Thelotornis kirtlandi*. Both of these snakes have fangs that are placed more forward in the mouth than in the other rear-fanged colubrids. In fact, their fangs are at their eye-level, similar to the location of the fangs in the elapids and viperids.

In all species of venomous snakes, fangs are shed regularly and are immediately replaced by new fangs that are growing behind the old ones. It is not unusual to see four or five replacement fangs available behind the fang that is in use.

Venom itself is a liquid mixture of numerous enzymes and proteins. Although in the past venom was characterized as neurotoxic, cytotoxic, cardiotoxic, or hemotoxic, it has been found that most snake venoms contain components that have all of these functions, although one or two toxin types may predominate. In general, venom of crotalines, the pit vipers (members of the viperid family), shows little neurotoxicity (damage to the nervous system) but many cytoxic (cell-destructive) effects in the area of the bite. Elapid venoms tend to have more of a neurotoxic component and some elapid venoms have cardiotoxic effects

SKULL OF REAR-FANGED BOOMSLANG (COLUBRID), *DISPHOLIDUS TYPUS*.

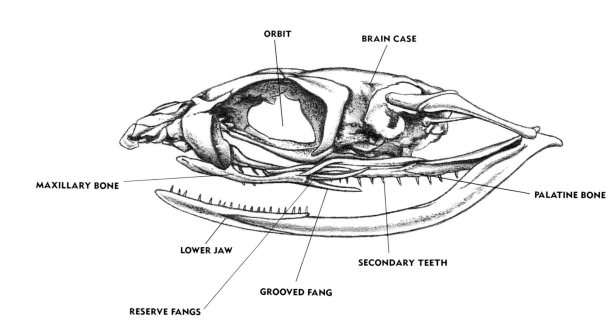

ORBIT

BRAIN CASE

MAXILLARY BONE

PALATINE BONE

LOWER JAW

SECONDARY TEETH

GROOVED FANG

RESERVE FANGS

ave venoms
and the pit
s vessels.

two corre-
cobras and
, 59, 60, 61,
rear-fanged
The venom
ar the most
ypodermic
ngs) are so
against the
ed; herein
which the
the venom
developed.
om glands
e ordinary
pparatus is
every few
lering the
enter the
e fixed in
overed by

ger" of a
The most
ape is en-

must find
e written
im might
unctures.
certain of
y Archi-
ite of its

56. Skeleton of a snake (Gaboon viper) showing the numerous ribs and bones of the back (vertebræ).

(Courtesy The American Museum of Natural History)

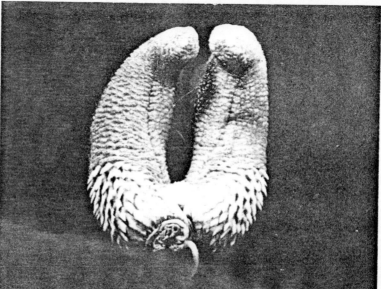

57. Penis of a snake (banded rattlesnake) in its functional position. This type is forked and has spines at the base. Each rattlesnake possesses two such organs.

(Photograph by Howard K. Gloyd, Chicago Academy of Sciences)

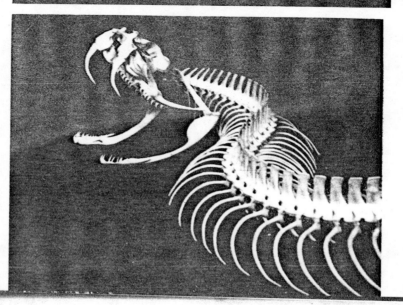

58. Skull of a viper (Gaboon viper) showing the two fangs (through which venom is injected) and the ordinary teeth of both upper (two rows) and lower (two rows) jaws. The reserve fangs, which will later replace the functional ones, can be clearly seen.

(Courtesy The American Museum of Natural History)

(damage to heart tissue) as well. According to Dr. Findlay Russell, one of the world's most knowledgeable snakebite experts, and his colleagues, snake venoms may contain many enzymes including proteinases, which destroy protein; L-arginine-ester hydrolases, which break down particular amino acid components; transaminase, which changes the structures of amino acids; hyaluronidase, which works on hyaluronic acid; L-amino acid oxidase, which breaks down certain amino acids; cholinesterase, an enzyme that destroys acetylcholine, a very important neurotransmitter that allows nerves to carry messages; phospholipases, which break down phospholipids, or the material that makes up the boundaries of the cells and of the small functioning components within the cell; ribonuclease, which breaks down ribonucleic acid; deoxyribonuclease, or DNase, which breaks down DNA or the genetic material; phosphomonoesterase and -diesterase, which move phosphate groups on molecules, especially molecules necessary for energy for the cell; ATPase, which breaks down adenosine triphosphate, or ATP, a molecule used for energy release in the cell; and more. From this list of enzymes, it is easy to see that venom injected into a human can wreak havoc upon the body, causing paralysis, suffocation, bleeding, tissue destruction, or vascular collapse. It is also clear from its components that the venom helps the snake digest its food. The proteinases break down proteins, the nucleases destroy the DNA and RNA, other chemicals change amino acids, and some help to digest fats. Interestingly, there may be variations in the types and amounts of components found in venoms from the same species of snakes living in different populations.

Snake venoms also contain toxins, many of which are produced exclusively by particular species or groups of species. Bungarotoxin, a powerful neurotoxic agent, is found in the venoms of *Bungarus*, the Asiatic and Indo-Australian kraits. Crotoxin is found in many species of crotaline snakes, the group that includes the rattlesnakes and copperheads of the United States. Mojave toxin is found specifically in the venom of the Mojave rattlesnake, *Crotalus s. scutulatus*. Vasoactive peptides, which may cause constriction or dilation of arterioles, also may be contained in venoms. Recent studies on some of the Middle Eastern atractaspids, which belong to their own family of venomous snakes, have characterized some of the toxic components in the venom. The potent toxins are called sarafotoxins and their major effects are on the heart itself and the coronary blood vessels supplying blood to the heart. Sarafotoxins increase contraction of heart muscle while at the same time blocking the electrical conduction system of the heart. Thus, the patient may die from fibrillation, where the two halves of the heart—upper and lower halves—beat independently and out of synchrony. Some of the toxins mimic the behavior of neurotransmitters and bind to the nerve endings, preventing messages from being sent from the brain to the periphery of the body and vice versa.

What happens to a person when he or she is bitten by a venomous snake? We consulted Dr. Warren Wetzel, director of the Trauma Service at Bronx Municipal Hospital Center and an associate professor of surgery at Albert Einstein College of Medicine in New York. Bronx Municipal Hospital Center has been designated as a regional snakebite treatment center, and as such, the center and Dr. Wetzel have treated forty-nine significant envenomations since 1981 and have consulted on many others. The most common bite seen in the United States is that of a pit viper, usually a rattlesnake. In the northeastern United States, bites from copperheads, a related crotaline, are also frequently seen. When a snakebite victim reaches the hospital, the emergency room team must first determine the species or, if the actual snake is not available or not known, the family of the snake that bit the patient. Often, especially when the bite has occurred outdoors, the patient or those accompanying the patient bring the snake (which they have probably killed) with them. If the

Vipers account for the majority of snakebites. Venom toxicity ranges from mildly dangerous, such as this Massasauga rattlesnake, *Sistrurus catenatus*, to highly toxic, which most often produces fatal results for the prey animal.

snake is an exotic snake from someone's private collection, the victim, friends, or family usually knows the species. Hospital personnel also need to know the time of the bite and the time of the onset of symptoms, if any.

According to Dr. Wetzel, a patient suffering from a pit viper bite is likely to have pain and localized swelling in the area of the bite as the earliest symptoms of envenomation. In bites by timber rattlesnakes, *Crotalus horridus horridus*, and some other crotalines, the patient may also experience a tingling sensation around the mouth. The patients are generally frightened and their anxiety produces hyperventilation (rapid breathing) and other symptoms that need to be sorted out from signs of envenomation. As with all trauma patients, the vital signs, that is, blood pressure, heart rate, respirations, urine output, and so on are recorded and continuously monitored. Any instability in the vital signs may indicate a severe envenomation that needs immediate aggressive treatment. Pit viper bites may lead to bleeding into the soft tissue, especially the tissue around the bite, and the patient's blood platelet count is routinely drawn to determine if there has been a loss of cells necessary for proper blood clotting. A significantly depressed platelet count is "one of the more important indicators of a severe bite," according to Dr. Wetzel. If the patient is not in a lot of pain and only shows a small amount of local tissue damage, he or she will be watched closely for progression of symptoms for the first thirty minutes after entering the emergency room. Many snakebites do not require anything other than supportive treatment. However, if symptoms progress significantly or are severe shortly after the bite, the standard treat-

The rodent-eating Wagler's viper, *Trimeresurus wagleri*, has huge venom glands, low-toxicity venom, and a mild disposition. This snake is often welcomed in temples and homes.

© John Visser

ment is to administer antivenin intravenously. Dr. Wetzel assured us that not all crotaline bites require antivenin. The least severe do not require any, but those that require antivenin treatment are obvious at the time the patient enters the hospital or become obvious shortly thereafter.

ANTIVENIN

Antivenin production is complicated and costly. Snake venom is collected by a handler who holds the snake and forces it to bite through a thin layer of material, often a paraffin film, wrapped over a jar. This procedure is called milking. Once venom is obtained it is injected into a horse. The horse's immune system reacts by producing antibodies to the venom. The next step is to extract blood from the horse. The serum containing the antibodies is separated from the rest of the blood, and the serum is purified so that it contains the specific antibodies and little else. This is antivenin. Unfortunately, antivenin manufactured in this manner still contains some horse proteins, and infusion of this substance into a human patient in most cases results in an allergic reaction to the horse serum. This is referred to as serum sickness. Serum sickness as a result of horse serum is no longer believed to be life threatening. The most serious allergic response is anaphylactic shock, and it can be controlled using epinephrine, antihistamines, and corticosteroid. Serum sickness can also be controlled with antihistamines and steroids, but it is extremely uncomfortable for the patient. Newer methods may allow antivenin production in sheep or in chicken eggs, which are much less allergenic than horse serum.

Sera produced in some of the Third World countries for treatment of elapid bites may be impure, or different batches may have different amounts of antibodies. Some batches may have so few active antibodies that they are useless in treating the bite. This is a serious problem, because although some antivenin may have an effect on the bites of many species of related snakes, a few of the Asiatic elapids require antivenin that is very specific.

A further problem with antivenin treatment, especially of bites from exotic snakes, is that antivenin for these bites may only be available from zoos that maintain these animals in their collections. Many hospitals in the United States, for example, stock small amounts of crotaline antivenin produced by Wyeth-Ayerst Laboratories, and Wyeth's staff is available twenty-four hours a

day to supply this antivenin to hospitals that need it in an emergency. There is, however, no call for most hospitals to stock antivenin against Australian tiger snake venom. An individual bitten by one of these snakes in New York and under treatment at Bronx Municipal Hospital Center may be lucky enough to obtain the antivenin from the Bronx zoo. A person bitten by one of these snakes from a private collection in a small city without a zoo may well be in a life-threatening situation.

Toronto General Hospital in Canada surveyed the local residents to find out what species of venomous snakes were held in captivity by people living in the area. The hospital now maintains enough antivenin of the required types to begin treatment in case any of these people are bitten by their pet snakes. Unfortunately, this system only works well as long as the pet owners comply and tell the truth about what species they maintain. Those who do not may be out of luck if their exotic venomous pet bites them and they are treated with the wrong antivenin or if no antivenin is available at all to treat the bite.

Although one might think that in North America elapid bites would only be seen in the southern United States, where coral snakes are found, or among zoo personnel, this is not the case. Dr. Wetzel has treated three cobra bites in New York City. Bites from elapids are frequent medical emergencies in Asia, Africa, and Australia. A patient who has sustained an elapid bite will show little tissue injury at the site of the bite, but may have neurological symptoms, such as slurred speech; drooling; numbness around the mouth, face, and bite site; and tingling around the bite site. Coral snakes, which are present in the southern United States, Mexico, and Central and South America, have a very slow-working venom. A victim of a coral snake bite may, at first, show no symptoms at all. Many coral snake bites result in no envenomation, as the snake has short fangs and needs to chew on the victim in order to inject venom. Neurological symptoms in coral snake envenomation, however, have an insidious onset and may lead to respiratory arrest and subsequent death if not treated. Thus, the rule of thumb in treating elapid bites is to treat with antivenin if there are any symptoms at all. Dr. Wetzel stressed that the only effective treatment for cobra bites is antivenin. A full dose of cobra venom, which is the amount injected in one bite, contains enough cardiotoxins to cause cardiac death and the only way to neutralize the toxins is to use cobra antivenin.

All snakebite victims should obtain medical treatment as soon as possible after the bite. Even in the United States, several people die every year as a result of venomous snakebite.

"Theoretically, we can successfully treat every snakebite," Dr. Wetzel stated, "yet every year several people in the United States die of envenomations. The deaths oftentimes are people who seek medical help very late or not at all." There are some people who are more likely to die of venomous snakebite, even with medical treatment, than the general population. These include people who have allergic reactions to the toxins in the venom, those with cardiovascular disease, those who are very ill, and those who are intoxicated. But for most people, obtaining emergency treatment as quickly as possible is the best way to survive a bite.

There are numerous statistics on the numbers of deaths worldwide from venomous snakebite, but no one seems to agree on the numbers, in part because many victims in Asia, Africa, and South America are in rural areas and die without receiving medical care. A conservative estimate is that 30,000 to 40,000 people per year die of the effects of venomous snakebite. Of these, 25,000 to 35,000 occur in Asia, 3,000 to 4,000 in South America, and the rest in Africa, North America, Europe, and Oceania, in that order. These figures may be wildly off. Julian White, Australia's preeminent snakebite authority, quotes sources indicating as many as 23,000 deaths may occur in West Africa, mostly resulting from the bite of the carpet viper, *Echis carinatus*. An Indian source complained that World Health Organization figures compiled in the mid-1950s indicating 20,000 deaths due to venomous snakebite annually in India are incorrect and that there really are about 9,000 deaths per year in India. Be that as it may, when compared with recent Australian figures, which are approximately two deaths per year, this number is massive.

According to White, the most venomous snakes in the world, in terms of venom toxicity, reside in Australia. The most dangerous venom in the world is that of the inland taipan, *Oxyuranus microlepidotus*, an Australian elapid. The next four most toxic venoms in the world are also from Australian snakes: the common brown snake, *Pseudonaja textilis*; the taipan, *Oxyuranus scutellatus*; the tiger snake, *Notechis scutatus*; and the Reevesby Island tiger snake, *Notechis ater niger*. A sea snake is next on the highly toxic list, followed by five more Australian elapids. If you look at both venom toxicity and amount of venom produced (the more venom produced the greater the dose of venom injected), the inland taipan is the most dangerous snake in the world, followed by the taipan, tiger snake, and death adder, *Acanthophis antarcticus*, another Australian elapid. But due to factors including fang length, aggressiveness of the snake, and human population distribution, these snakes are responsible for few fatal bites compared to the carpet viper of Africa and Russell's viper, *Vipera russelli*, of Asia. These snakes are numerous and inhabit heavily populated areas—even some cities.

© Rom Whitaker

The taipan, left, *Oxyuranus scutellatus*, is considered the most deadly of snakes due to its very highly neurotoxic venom that kills by rapid paralysis of the nervous system. An attacking taipan often hurls itself with a short hissing growl at an intruder. The fine quality antiserum produced in Australia is often the only difference between life and death after a bite. The inland taipan, below, *Oxyuranus microlepidotus*, has the most toxic venom of any snake.

© Julian White

Victims of bites from Australian elapids tend to show typical neurotoxin effects, including loss of consciousness and progressive paralysis. They may suffer from improper blood clotting mechanisms and may show muscle destruction. According to White, in Australia, the group most at risk for venomous snakebite is toddlers 1 to 3 years of age. The danger lies partly in the children's curiosity and partly in the common occurrence of juvenile venomous brown snakes *Pseudonaja* species. Males, both in children and adults, tend to be victims more often than females. White is of the same opinion as Dr. Warren Wetzel: immediate treatment is the best way to avoid fatality or complications from the bite of any venomous Australian snake. As he stated in an article on management of snakebite, ". . . death from snake bite in Australia should be rare."

AVOIDING SNAKEBITE

The obvious way to avoid being bitten by a venomous snake is to avoid all possible contacts with snakes. This would mean having to live in the polar regions or a few select places on earth. At the very least, one would have to give up going outdoors except, perhaps, in large cities. Yet who would be willing to give up the wonderful experiences that visits to the outdoors hold? Most people enjoy being exposed to wildlife in all of its natural beauty, and neither harm nature nor are harmed by it.

The incidence of snakebite around the world is very low. Even among people who live in remote or rural communities, in places where venomous snakes abound, and where their daily lives place them in contact with venomous snakes, deaths from snakebite are unusual or rare. Needless to say, the incidence of snakebite among a million people in a major city is going to be significantly lower than the incidence of snakebite among the rural inhabitants of an Indian village, where nocturnal vipers and elapids are plentiful and where people sleep on the floor in crude houses that are easily invaded. In the United States, approximately 8,000 people are bitten annually, yet there are only between nine and fifteen fatalities, some of which might have been avoided if appropriate treatment was quickly sought. Oddly enough, there are significant numbers of snakebites occurring each year in major cities such as New York and Washington, D.C. Many of these are from exotic Asian and African vipers and cobras. In fact, in the Northeast, the accidental snakebite incurred by a hiker or picnicker is rare.

Interestingly, the typical snakebite victim in the United States is a male between the ages of seventeen and forty, and in most cases, he is under the influence of alcohol or other substances. The vast majority of snakebites are received by people who are attempting to capture or kill a snake, and a large number are inflicted on those who keep venomous snakes as pets, often illegally. Venomous pet snakes account for almost all exotic snakebites in cities excluding bites of zoo personnel (which are extremely rare).

The consequences of harboring a venomous snake in a private collection are enormous and far reaching. Even the most cautious and experienced professional snake keeper recognizes that a mishap can occur at any time, with even the slightest error in judgment and with the best of facilities. That the most dangerous of venomous snakes in the greatest numbers are cared for daily by the herpetology staffs of zoological parks, with rarely a snakebite accident, is a fact that speaks for itself.

Should a snakebite occur in an institutional collection, the staff is well prepared. There is a well-defined snakebite and emergency-response protocol already in place. The appropriate antivenin is on hand in sufficient quantities. An affiliation with a local hospital and emergency room staff is often established to be sure that hospital personnel are familiar with the treatment

The tropical rattlesnake, *Crotalus durissus*. The deep facial pit located between the eye and the nostrils readily identifies the New World pit vipers. Not all venomous snakes are as easy to identify.

protocol and the medical histories of the people at risk. The Herpetology Department of the New York Zoological Society has been a leader in developing snakebite accident protocols for professional institutions. The result is that a snakebite victim in a zoological institution generally experiences the bite during normal working hours when communications, designated treatment staff, and transportation are at their best. Proper first aid is initiated immediately by trained personnel, and the victim is under hospital treatment within minutes, receiving appropriate antivenin by an experienced physician.

In contrast, the victim who receives a venomous snakebite in a private collection is at a great disadvantage and considerably greater risk. The bite has a much higher chance of resulting in damage, possible loss of appendages, and even death. The bite often occurs at night, alcohol or other incapacitating substances are often involved, and the victim does not know what to do and panics. Because harboring the venomous snake may be against local laws and the victim is open to prosecution, the victim's first inclination may be to try to hide the bite and hope it gets better on its own. It will not. Instead, precious time is lost as the symptoms increase. Excessive bleeding, swelling, and rapid discoloration of the bite area, intense increasing pain, nausea, dizziness, fainting, muscle twitches, and difficulty in breathing may follow envenomation. When the victim finally seeks help at the emergency room of a local hospital, he will, if conscious, often make up a story about what happened, hoping to avoid admitting illegal ownership of the snake. In doing so, he professes not to know what species of snake inflicted the bite or how it got there. This is a grave error, as antivenins are often specific for certain snakes or groups, and the physician must apply the appropriate treatment for the type of venom, depending on the species involved. The local hospital physician on duty is not expecting to have to treat a snakebite in the small hours of his or her tour in a city hospital, perhaps far removed from snakes. The snake involved may well be an exotic species that can inflict a mortal bite in a few hours, and the physician suddenly must start learning about snakebite. More time is lost and the patient may deteriorate rapidly. If the victim is lucky, the doctor may have been put in contact with experienced personnel at another hospital who can advise on how to stabilize the victim and transport the victim to a prepared facility, if possible. Unfortunately, in some cases, treatments for bites from common local species are initially administered, which may actually make the situation worse, as they compound the effects of the venom of some exotic snakes. Other than zoological institutions that stock sufficient sera for the protection of their own staff, antivenins for treating exotic snakebites are not readily available and are not stocked by hospitals. The serum, once located and if available, must then be transported to the hospital and the victim, often many hours away.

The best advice on the keeping and handling of venomous snakes is DO NOT. The potential hazard to the owner is considerable and the consequences, both legal and traumatic, involving an unsuspecting victim should the snake escape and bite someone, are great indeed.

There is little reason for anyone to capture wild venomous snakes for other than scientific purposes for a scientific institution. Photograph them and leave them undisturbed, as you find them.

That said, if we are to introduce our children to nature and make them aware and appreciative of wildlife, we must include snakes, as we would any other kind of animal. First of all, children should be taught to leave all snakes alone unless they are with a responsible adult who has the knowledge to identify the species in that region. Start the introduction with one of the excellent field guides that are readily available in book shops and libraries. Next, find out what zoo or nature camp has exhibits that include local species. Bring your field guide and compare the snakes on exhibit to the illustrations. You may want to talk to the keeper in charge of the snake collection and ask specific questions about hard-to-identify types. Most professional herpetologists are eager to talk with young people and help them in their interest, as long as they indicate their willingness to pursue that interest in a safe and responsible way.

A few general rules apply whether you are looking for snakes to photograph or observe or are simply taking a hike through the countryside. Bear in mind that snakes frequent different types of habitats in different regions of the world. Talk to local people who will know. What holds true for the eastern United States may not be true in Australia or in South America. It is important to know what species frequent the particular region you are visiting and which are the nocturnal and diurnal species and which are apt to be about at any time.

A primary rule is never put your hands or your feet where you cannot see. Most snakes can only strike about a third of their body length, but a snake on a downhill slope or a particularly aggressive animal may lunge its entire body length or more in some instances.

During the heat of the day, most snakes will hide in the shade of bushes, thickets, and underground litter or in rock crevices. Watch where you are walking. Always wear long pants and sturdy leather walking boots that come up as high on the leg as possible. Snakes strike at what they see (and, in the cases of pit

vipers and boas, what they sense, using their infrared and heat sensors) and what disturbs them and moves. If your leg is exposed, it will be the target. Baggy pants are a better target. While a rattlesnake or other viper can penetrate canvas, rubber, and most leather, knee-high rubber or leather boots do provide considerable protection. For people at particular risk by virtue of their occupations, several manufacturers produce high boots made from elk hide and leggings and canvas brush pants made with laminated wire mesh that are snakeproof.

Try to avoid walking near crevasses in rocks or climbing down rock faces. Your head and body especially should not be exposed to the strike of a basking or hidden snake. Bites to these parts of the body are exceptionally dangerous.

Do not blindly step over fallen logs. A snake may lie hidden in the shade of the underside of the log. Walk around it or step onto the log, and look carefully on the other side before stepping down. Be especially careful about sitting on fallen logs for the same reasons. The exposed part of your body is not only a large target but a bite to the buttocks is most embarrassing. Look carefully and train your eyes to see snakes as they lie camouflaged. If in doubt, thrust around the site with a stick. This often disturbs an unseen snake into moving and gives the snake's hiding place away.

Do not sleep on the ground where snakes occur. Snakes have been known to crawl under or onto a sleeping person. Nocturnal venomous snakes in rural India have bitten sleeping people. Sleep on a platform or use a hammock. Such a precaution will also help you avoid sharing your blankets with scorpions and other unwelcome visitors. If you have to walk about at night, wear long pants and boots. Use a good flashlight or headlamp and keep it trained about six feet (2 m) in front of you and stay away from the brushy margins of a path. Think about where you are walking. A friend of ours in India walked off his porch one night to see what the dogs were barking at and nearly stepped on a large viper immediately in front of his house.

When traveling by car through narrow brush-lined roads in regions where arboreal venomous snakes may bask in low branches, keep your arms inside. More than one person has been bitten as their arm dislodged a basking snake.

Be particularly cautious around old buildings and sheds. Snakes frequent places where rodents abound and often stay close to or inside such places because of the food supply.

Basically, use good common sense in areas where snakes are encountered; don't touch or try to handle snakes you do not know; don't keep poisonous snakes as pets.

© John Visser

Freeze-dried venom extracted from an endemic venomous species is the first step in the production of anti-venin. The venom's toxicity remains potent for many years if properly stored.

SNAKES AND HUMANS

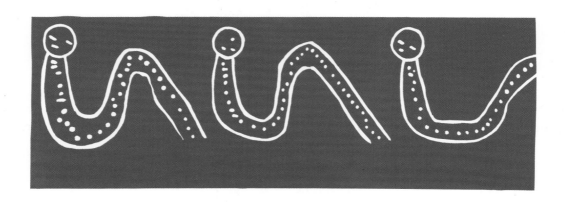

People are terrified of snakes. Carry a snake into any fourth-grade classroom and you will observe the typical reaction of our species to snakes. Half the class, not always the girls, will shriek, and some children will run into corners or under desks, hiding as far from the offending creature as possible. Two or three children will show an almost morbid interest, and the remainder will be interested, but slightly apprehensive. If any adults are present, half of them will be obviously terrified and the remainder will behave exactly as teachers should behave . . . like adults who are in control.

Why are we so terrified of snakes? One herpetologist insists that we learn this behavior from our mothers. I recently saw a large, powerful man reduced to a shivering mass of jelly when he raked up a small brown Dekay's snake with the leaves. I asked him if his mother had been afraid of snakes. He explained to me that his family came from the southern United States, where snakes were very common and his mother used to catch snakes—grab them by the tail, whip them around, and smash their heads. "She wasn't afraid of anything," he said. So be it for the mother theory.

Higher primates in zoos appear to be terrified of snakes, screaming and yelling and jumping up and down when snakes are around. Is this a genetic behavior pattern? Have we inherited a fight-or-flight response to the sight of a long slinky body with an arrowlike head? How can we be afraid of typhlopids, the blind worm snakes, some half the width of our pinkie? Are we afraid of earthworms? (Kids may say, "Ooh, yuck," but they'll pick them up.) There is no answer. Freud and many others equate the snake to the phallus, but human reproduction patterns indicate that any societal fear of the male sex organ is readily overcome.

We invest snakes with foul behavior patterns and bad motives. As proof we need only look to the snake in the Adam and Eve story. In fact, the ancient Hebrews, with whom this story developed, were well acquainted with snakes, some of which were extremely dangerous. We use the phrase, "a snake in the grass" to refer to someone who is devious, but "a snake in

The Dekay's snake, *Storeria dekayi*, is a common inhabitant of suburban gardens and flower beds in the eastern and central United States, where it feeds on earthworms and slugs.

the grass" is likely to be on its way to its next rodent meal, helping humans by keeping destructive rodent populations down. Being serpent-tongued may mean that you "speak with forked tongue," not a very good thing to do, but almost all snakes are mute and their tongues are sensory organs, certainly not used in vocalizations. In the Indiana Jones series of movies, there is an obligatory snake scene. The audience writhes. It is repellent. But why? Would a room full of dogs make your skin crawl as much?

If someone loses a pet snake, especially a large one, like a boa constrictor, it is news. The local TV station may cover it, and there will be a few lines, at the very least, in the newspaper, even in a big city. But if my Great Dane runs away, although it is probably as rare a pet as a boa and a lot bigger and more dangerous, too, I would be lucky to get one sentence into my local block association's newsletter. There are people who will not even enter my house because they are afraid of a caged kingsnake in my son's room. Rather than a "Beware of Dog" sign on my house, I often think of putting up a sign that reads, "We Keep Snakes" as a deterrent to burglars!

SNAKES AND CULTURE

When one thinks of the cultural uses of snakes, snake charming tends to come to mind. We generally think of snake charming as a strictly Indian cultural institution, but snake charmers are found

in many areas of southeast Asia and Africa. Although the usual snake we think of being "charmed" is a cobra, other species, both venomous and non-venomous, are used. Snake charming, in fact, is a ruse. The late Jim Oliver, who was Curator of Reptiles at the New York Zoological Park in the 1950s, discussed snake charming in his book, *Snakes in Fact and Fiction*. Although snakes are not deaf, they do not hear high-pitched airborne sounds and certainly cannot respond to the intricacies of song. Snakes do, however, respond to visual messages of movement. Thus, it is the flute's movement that the snake follows, giving the impression that it is being "charmed." Cobras respond to snake charming with a head up and hood flattened posture. Unlike many snakes that strike outward from a tightly coiled S shape, cobras strike downward, the tip of the snout etching a quarter circle in the air with the outstretched head and upper body serving as the radius of the circle. A snake charmer can avoid a bite by remaining slightly beyond the distance at which the head can strike. To avoid any risk, however, snakes used by snake charmers are often mutilated so that venom cannot be injected. Some charmers sew the snakes' mouths closed. There are stories of entire families in India contributing to the snake charming work by sewing the snakes' mouths closed. Obviously, a snake with a sewn mouth eventually starves to death. Other snakes have both their primary and reserve fangs removed, most by crude surgical techniques. Many of these snakes develop mouth and venom gland infections and die shortly thereafter. Some are either milked of venom or fed a meal (during which they inject venom into prey) immediately prior to the performance so that they have less than a full dose of venom to inject. The end result of all but the last of these techniques is that the snakes are soon discarded and replaced with new ones.

Dr. Oliver reported on the famous snake dance of the Hopis, a native American group of the southwestern United States. The snake dance itself is part of a nine-day religious ritual performed in August that probably is related to the harvest, especially the harvest of corn. Corn was an important staple food of the Hopis. Snakes live in cornfields and eat the rodents that destroy corn, so the significance of snakes to the survival of the Hopi people was very great. During the snake dance, priests carry snakes in their mouths and hands, apparently without sustaining bites. Although not all snakes included in the snake dance are venomous, many rattlesnakes are used. The question of why the snake dancers did not appear to be bitten or envenomated excited a lot of speculation among herpetologists during the latter part of the nineteenth and the early part of the twentieth centuries. Some snakes obtained and examined after snake dances showed both the fangs and reserve fangs to have been neatly excised from the jaws. The herpetologists assumed that, at least by the early part of this century, the snakes were rendered harmless by this surgical procedure. Prior to that time, they assumed that the snakes may have been milked or fed immediately prior to the dance.

Among the oddest contemporary involvements with venomous snakes are the snake cults of the southeastern United States. Begun in the early 1900s by a man named George Went Hensley, the cults, in typical revival meeting style, take quite seriously the biblical passage from Mark 16, "They shall take up serpents," handling snakes in their rites. Weston La Barre's book, not so coincidentally named *They Shall Take Up Serpents*, explored the psychological reasons people join these snake cults. People sometimes are bitten during the snake handling rituals. Sometimes they survive and sometimes they die from the bite. Between 1945 and 1989, there were eleven known deaths among cult followers in West Virginia due to venomous snakebite. Unfortunately, those who are bitten repeatedly and survive may build up immunity to the effects of the toxins and may therefore survive future bites, which encourages members of the cult who have not yet been bitten to believe that they, too, can be bitten and survive as a result of divine intervention. Although law enforcement officials certainly frown on and may even forbid such dangerous shows, the cults persist in handling snakes.

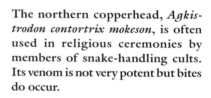

The northern copperhead, *Agkistrodon contortrix mokeson*, is often used in religious ceremonies by members of snake-handling cults. Its venom is not very potent but bites do occur.

© Sharon Cummings/Dembinsky Photo Associates

SNAKES AND MEDICINE

There is a long history of snake tissues, organs, and products being used for medicinal purposes. Historically, snake skins, gallbladders, oil, and flesh all had numerous medicinal uses. The ancient Greeks believed snakeskins tied around a pregnant woman's abdomen would make childbirth faster and less painful. The fat from a snake was supposed to be an aid to conception. In the seventeenth century, upper-class women believed that feasting on viper meat would improve the quality of their skin. Even today we speak of "snake oil" salesmen, selling dubious cure-alls in a bottle. In parts of Southeast Asia, snake gallbladders are prized for their curative powers.

The truth is less positive, but somewhat promising. To date, there are no medically proven drugs or pharmaceuticals made from snakes or snake products, although this does not prevent people from believing that snakes have curative powers.

A recent study of cases of apparent food poisoning among Latinos in Los Angeles resulted in the strange finding that these people had ingested capsules containing dried, ground rattlesnake meat, which happened to be contaminated with the *Salmonella* bacterium. They obtained the capsules in Mexico, Central America, and even pharmacies in Los Angeles and took them in the false belief that they would cure "AIDS, arthritis, blood disorders, cancer, infections, itchy feet, sinus and skin conditions, and diarrhea."

Of all snake products, venoms hold the most promise as pharmaceuticals, because they contain unique and highly complex proteins and bioactive substances. Although there are no drugs presently made from snake venoms, their unique qualities, especially those of the neurotoxic venoms, which bind to nerve endings or the neuromuscular junction, have led to scientific discoveries related to the workings of the nervous system. Venoms also are used in studies of cell membrane structure and function. It is hoped that someday portions of these venoms may be used to slow or prevent the progression of such neurological and muscular diseases as muscular dystrophy and multiple sclerosis, among others. For now, venoms and their components are used experimentally. There is, however, one commercial medical diagnostic product that utilizes components of snake venoms. Reptilase®-PC is a test kit distributed in the United States by Bio/Data Corporation of Hatboro, Pennsylvania, used to determine blood clot formation times in patients treated with anticoagulant drugs. The test is often used post-surgically as it reveals clotting abnormalities in the blood. It uses an extract of the venom of *Bothrops atrox*, a South and Central American pit viper (crotaline). *Bothrops* venom contains substances that lead to coagulopathies, or abnormal blood coagulation. They are potent clot inducers and cause the formation of numerous small blood clots throughout the circulatory system, using up the clotting factors, and leaving the patient with insufficient clotting factors to prevent massive internal and external bleeding. (This is a case in which too much of one thing leads to its opposite effect.)

TRADE, UTILIZATION, AND CONSERVATION OF SNAKES

While it is relatively easy to generate public interest and concern for the protection and conservation of cuddly soft mammals and brightly colored birds, most people harbor the attitude of "Who needs snakes?" Yet snakes not only play a useful role in our environment, but are important members of the ecological community.

Crossed pit viper or urutu, *Bothrops alternatus.*

The major threats to snake populations vary from one part of the world to another and from species to species. Many snake species are so highly specialized that any disruption in the food chain dramatically affects them. Aquatic species are highly vulnerable to pollution from toxic wastes. Insectivorous species and those that feed on centipedes, for instance, are particularly affected by efforts to control insects through the widespread use of toxic chemicals such as DDT, nicotine sprays, and other pesticides.

Loss of habitat through agricultural development, habitat modification, and the inroads of expanding human populations are primary factors adversely affecting most species. While some species may actually adapt to some habitat modifications and find new sources of food, others cannot and perish. Unfortunately, some of the species that adapt well are also venomous and dangerous to humans. In some instances, mammal-eating species initially do well with the coming of people because humans often bring poverty and poor sanitary conditions, which encourage rodents to proliferate. Some snakes, such as cobras, *Naja*, are quick to take advantage of this newfound ready source of food. While the snakes remain hidden during the day, when people are about, the cobras feed at night. Thus their contact with humans is diminished, that is, until the human numbers and their homes and streets become better developed and the snakes have fewer places to retreat. Reticulated pythons, *Python reticulatus*, and even king cobras, *Ophiophagus hannah*, are known to be found occasionally in the storm drains and natural areas within the suburbs and city limits of Singapore in recent times. Kraits, *Bungarus*, cobras, *Naja*, and coral snakes, *Micrurus*, frequently live in and around old buildings and rural habitations in many regions of the world.

One of the most serious threats to many snake species is the wholesale killing of snakes for commercial purposes, for their skins, supposed medicinal properties, meat, and sport. The number of snakes killed commercially is difficult to assess. Dr. C. Kenneth Dodd of the U.S. Fish and Wildlife Service, who is particularly concerned about the decline of many snake populations around the world, cites World Wildlife Fund figures that indicate that for a three-month period in 1982, over $3.2 million dollars' worth of Asian whipsnake, *Ptyas mucosus*, skins alone were imported into the United States. During this period, snakeskin products were being touted as the fashion of the season. Millions upon millions of snakes are killed each year for the luxury exotic leather trade, often in violation of national and international wildlife regulations. The giant snakes, boas and pythons, are particularly subject to skin-trade decimations. Oddly enough, snake leather is one of the poorest of leathers in

terms of durability and wear. It generally needs to be backed with domestic leathers to give it thickness. Soon after use, scales often begin to upturn and fray, giving the handbag or shoes a poor look. Snake farms exist in Brazil, India, and Africa, among other places. However, these exist generally for the entertainment of tourists and the extraction of venom for use in the preparation of anti-snakebite sera. New animals are continually supplied from wild populations rather than from captive reproduction. No farms exist in the world for the breeding of snakes for their skins. Some farms that profess to do so are largely clearinghouses for animals taken from the wild.

The use of snake products for medicine and aphrodisiacs also takes its toll on populations. In parts of southern China and in Southeast Asian countries with large ethnic Chinese populations, snake gallbladders are taken for use as medicine to cure numerous ills, and snake gallbladder and blood concoctions are drunk to increase sexual potency. (Back to the old phallus myth.)

Although cobras, *Naja*, are responsible for many deaths in India, their great value in controlling rodents has led the Indian government to place them under strictest protection.

© John Visser

It is impossible to account for the millions of snakes that are killed for this purpose. During the 1800s in the United States, snake oil cures for arthritis became the trademark of hucksters and other nefarious traders.

There are limited, but legitimate, uses for snake venom in scientific research. Some of the venoms block transmission of nerve impulses and, as such, are an important tool in studying neurophysiology and functions of anesthetics. A number of years ago, a study was begun on effects of snake venom on progression of a debilitating neurological disease, but the work was discontinued. As more is learned about the structure and function of snake venoms, it is likely that they may have further uses in medical research and perhaps even in treating disease.

A surprisingly large number of snakes are taken from the wild each year for the exotic pet trade. Thousands of snakes of every description and size, venomous and nonvenomous alike, are imported into North America and Europe from Asia, Africa, and South America for amateur snake collectors' private collections. Some snake-breeding farms have sprung up in Colombia, South America, for boa constrictors and other reptiles that are commonly found on the pet markets of the world. Colombia and Ecuador were primary suppliers of reptile pets for the trade for many years. By the mid 1970s, it became nearly impossible to find reptiles, or any other types of wildlife utilized for the pet trade, for several days' journey in the regions surrounding major air shipping points.

Dozens of snakebites are reported each year from urban hospitals. Generally, the bites are not inflicted on campers and wilderness hikers who happen upon native venomous species, but rather on amateur herpetologists who are bitten by their own exotic, often very dangerous, pet. No comprehensive national or international bans exist to prohibit the importation of venomous species, except for those species listed under Appendix I, II, or III of the Convention on the International Trade in Endangered Species (CITES) or under national laws such as the U.S. Endangered Species Act and the U.S. Lacey Act, which also prohibits U.S. citizens from engaging in trade in United States–listed endangered species anywhere in the world. Prohibitions related to keeping these dangerous pets presently fall under a patchwork of local municipal, state, or provincial regulations.

The United Kingdom, Canada, and Australia, for example, all are signatories of CITES and all have various internal regulations governing the import, export, and keeping of snakes in captivity. In all of these countries, CITES permits must be in hand before any endangered species can be imported or exported. But only a very few of the venomous or dangerous snakes people maintain in their personal collections are endangered species, while many more, acquired from the wild, may originate from protected sources. Australia and its states and territories have very stringent laws on both possession and export of native reptiles. Permits are only issued to zoos and other scientific institutions for scientific purposes only. In Canada, laws vary from province to province, but endangered species laws and even laws on transshipment of nonendangered snakes from the United States to Canada are often enforced with difficulty. An endangered snake from a country other than the United States requires a CITES and an Agriculture of Canada approval or permit. A snake brought in from the United States requires a CITES permit if the snake is listed on one of the CITES appendices or, if not, a proof of purchase. A person wishing to bring a snake obtained legally or otherwise in the United States into Canada often just puts the snake in a bag in the car and drives across the border without declaring the snake. This is a major importation method, and the United States—Canada route is a

Boa constrictors, *Boa constrictor*, are probably the best-known pet snake. Although many of the pet boa constrictors are bred in captivity, millions of snakes of many species are taken from the wild annually for the commercial pet trade and the snake leather industry.

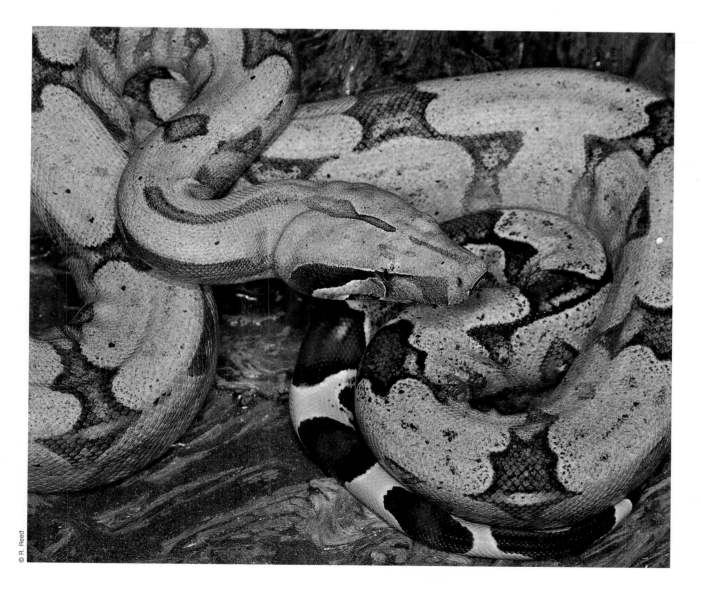

major route for illegal importation of snakes into Canada. In Ontario, it is illegal to maintain a number of species of native snakes as pets. The eastern massasauga, *Sistrurus catenatus catenatus*, a small rattlesnake, is listed as endangered and may not be kept in Ontario. The Canadian black rat snake, *Elaphe obsoleta obsoleta*, may not be kept legally in Ontario, but a snake of the same species obtained in Pennsylvania may be brought into Canada and kept as a pet in Ontario if the owner can supply proof of purchase from a seller in Pennsylvania. In the United Kingdom, venomous snakes and other dangerous reptiles are banned from private possession by the Dangerous Wild Animal Act, although Britain has no laws preventing you from maintaining other non-dangerous, non-endangered snakes as pets. Thus, you can see how complicated the mass of regulations regarding the import, export, and keeping of snakes can be.

In most areas, laws focus on minimal prosecution for harboring a dangerous animal, often only after a complaint is made or an accident occurs. Many snake fanciers and private collectors breed many species of snakes for sale or trade. The actual number of snakes in private captivity is unknown. Many professionally minded snake collectors have formed clubs and associations in order to give responsible guidance to young people, discourage the keeping of dangerous species, and encourage the conservation and protection of endangered species. Anyone interested in

Snake fanciers now breed many rare exotic species. Yellow and red, green tree python, *Chondropython viridis*, babies are highly desired and command hundreds of U.S. dollars each.

such organizations should contact the herpetology department of their local zoo, museum, or university.

Some speculative concern has been voiced that along with other wildlife species, climatic global warming trends have adversely affected some species of snakes, especially those that are endemic to temperate regions. No studies have yet been done.

Decimations of many snake species have led state wildlife authorities to pass regulations prohibiting the capturing or killing of endemic species of snakes. Due to concern over declining populations, even venomous species such as the timber rattlesnake, *Crotalus horridus*, and the eastern Massasauga, *Sistrurus catenatus*, have received protection as endangered species in a number of northeastern states, and many western species of rattlesnakes that have limited distributions have received protection as well.

As of 1990, at least thirty-six individual species and several entire families of snakes are the subject of regulation or international protection through CITES listings. Fourteen species of snakes are specifically listed as endangered or threatened species under the United States' Endangered Species Act. A number of countries include snakes in total bans on taking wildlife for commercial purposes. India, as a leading example, recognized the great service snakes provided in controlling disease-transmitting rats and other rodents and listed species such as the whipsnake, *Ptyas*, and common cobra, *Naja naja*, under its protections, despite the significant number of human deaths due to snakebite attributed to the latter species each year in that country. Hunting for the commercial skin trade was rapidly decimating cobra and whipsnake populations. The declines were associated with an alarming increase in rats, human health problems, and destruction of grain stores.

The problems faced by wildlife authorities in protecting snake species are enormous. Public apathy, large profits in skin trading, enormous volumes of skins and products, limited scientific literature on the species found in many regions, and a lack of forensic methods for identifying protected species when they are manufactured into hides and products are major obstacles.

© John Visser

© John Visser

© R. Reed

Opposite, top

Family: Typhlopidae
Common Name: Braminy worm
snake or flowerpot snake
Scientific Name: *Typhlina* (also
Rhamphotyphlops) *bramina*
Location: Circumtropical
(throughout the world);
introduced into the New World

These small, blind snakes, rarely
larger than 7 inches (17 cm), are
thought to be the only known par-
thenogenic snake species, reproduc-
ing without a male. Only female
specimens have been found, and it is
thought that males do not exist.

Opposite, bottom

Family: Typhlopidae
Common Name: Bibron's blind
snake
Scientific Name: *Typhlops bibronii*
Location: Eastern South Africa
with one small population in
eastern Zimbabwe

This is a stout-bodied worm snake
averaging 14 to 15 inches (35 to 38
cm). The largest specimens are 18
inches (46 cm). Eyes are reduced
and scales are smooth to facilitate
burrowing.

Above

Family: Leptotyphlopidae
Common Name: Slender thread
snake
Scientific Name: *Leptotyphlops
gracilior*
Location: Small area in western
South Africa

These are incredibly thin burrowing snakes that may reach 9.5 inches
(24 cm) in length. The diet of all
African members of the genus consists of termites. A pheromone, or
hormonelike substance, is secreted
externally and prevents attacks by
soldier termites.

© R. Reed

© John Visser

Opposite, top

Family: Boidae
Common Name: Brazilian rainbow boa
Scientific Name: *Epicrates cenchria cenchria*
Location: The Amazon River basin, South America

A moderate-size (6 to 7 feet [1.8 to 2.0 m]), powerful constrictor that is well adapted to nocturnal hunting with sensory pits around the lips. Its name is derived from the iridescent blue-green sheen of its skin. This snake is not well tempered and frequently coils itself into a ball if disturbed.

Opposite, bottom

Family: Boidae
Common Name: Malagasy ground boa
Scientific Name: *Acrantophis madagascariensis*
Location: Madagascar

Reaching 10 feet (3 m) in length, this relatively short-tailed constrictor inhabits open forests. It feeds on small mammals and birds during the warm-weather months of the year. It hibernates during the colder months. The live-born young are quite large—as long as 2 feet (.6 m).

Below

Family: Boidae
Common Name: Yellow anaconda
Scientific Name: *Eunectes notaeus*
Location: The grasslands of southern Brazil, Bolivia, Paraguay, and northern Argentina

This is the anaconda of the Pantanal grasslands of Brazil. It reaches up to 15 feet (4.6 m) in length. A favorite food is the yacaré caiman, which it quickly seizes at the base of the skull to keep from being bitten by the caiman's powerful jaws. It quickly kills the caiman by constriction. It is a highly aquatic species and is widely hunted for its skin for the leather trade.

This page, top and bottom

Family: Boidae
Common Name: Emerald tree boa
Scientific Name: *Corallus canina*
Location: The Amazon River basin

Juvenile emerald tree boas, top, are rusty red to blue-green in color at birth and soon after begin to take on the bright green-and-white pattern of the adult (bottom). Adult emerald tree boas often appear enameled with white cross bands on the back with a brilliant bright green base color. These snakes are highly arboreal and they rarely are visible due to their cryptic coloration. Active at night, the snakes spend their days draped in characteristic body loops. Armed with profuse thermal receptors and exceptionally long front teeth adapted for piercing through feathers and holding birds, they are a most proficient nocturnal hunter.

(*Photograph by Isabelle Hunt Conant*)

77. Emerald tree boa (*Boa canina*).

© David T. Roberts

© Rom Whitaker

This page, top

Family: Boidae
Common Name: Central American dwarf boa
Scientific Name: *Ungaliophis panamensis*
Location: Rain forests of southern Central America to eastern Colombia
   This small, rare boa apparently does not exceed about 30 inches (.8 m) in length. It is thought to feed on lizards, frogs, and small mammals, and occasionally take birds. Little is known of its habits.

This page, bottom

Family: Boidae
Common Name: Whitaker's sand boa
Scientific Name: *Eryx whitakeri*
Location: Reported to be an Indian species
   Named after and by the famed herpetologist, Romulus Whitaker, this species probably does not exceed 30 inches (.8 m) in length. Like other sand boas, the species probably spends most of its time burrowed under loose sand.

This page, top

Family: Boidae
Common Name: Rubber boa
Scientific Name: *Charina bottae*
Location: Western United States to southern Canada

This small boid rarely exceeds 30 inches (.8 m) in length. It feeds on small rodents, which it hunts in burrows and termite mounds. Its name is derived from the limp, rubbery feel of its body. It is an innocuous species and will roll into a ball and present its tail to an intruder rather than strike.

This page, bottom

Family: Boidae
Common Name: Rosy boa
Scientific Name: *Lichanura trivirgata*
Location: Southwestern United States and Baja California

This species and the rubber boa are the only two boid species that are native to the United States. This species, however, lives in deserts and drier areas, although it also occurs around cultivated agricultural developments. It is nocturnal. The young are large—about 12 inches (30 cm) long when born. It eats small rodents and lizards.

Opposite

Family: Pythonidae
Common Name: Angolan python
Scientific Name: *Python anchietae*
Location: Southwest Africa including parts of Angola and Namibia

This is a small python that grows to about 5 to 6 feet (1.5 to 1.8 m) in length. One of the most attractively patterned python species, it lives on rocky hillsides as well as moister open areas with scrub. Not much is known of the species' habits. It feeds on small mammals and birds.

Family: Pythonidae
Common Name: Burmese python
Scientific Name: *Python molurus bivittatus*
Location: Southeast Asia and Indo-Australian Archipelago

Despite its name, this inhabitant of lush forests and moist lowlands is not restricted to Burma (currently Myanmar). It attains lengths of 26 feet (8 m). Burmese pythons spend much of their time in the water and are good swimmers. They are capable of feeding on larger mammals but often eat ground-dwelling birds. This species is unique in being able to regulate its body temperature by several degrees during egg incubation. Between 60 and 100 leathery-shelled white eggs are laid in a secluded tree hollow or other sheltered spot. This snake is widely killed for its skin and is often bred for the pet trade.

Family: Pythonidae
Common Name: Blood python
Scientific Name: *Python curtus*
Location: Southeast Asia

This short, stout python frequents a highly aquatic environment that includes swamps and streams within rain forests. While individuals may occasionally reach 6 feet (1.8 m) in length, most animals are much shorter than that but the body girth may be as great as 6 inches (15 cm) in diameter. Some individuals are blood red in color (hence, the common name), while others are bright orange and yellow. This animal is quick to strike and feeds mostly on small mammals and birds. The female incubates and protects the 6 to 12 large eggs by coiling around them throughout the incubation period.

Family: Pythonidae
Common Name: Ball python or royal python
Scientific Name: *Python regius*
Location: West Africa

This small inhabitant of fields and grasslands is the African counterpart of the Asian blood python. Rarely reaching 5 feet (1.5 m) in length, this powerful constrictor immediately forms its body into a tight ball when attacked. So strong is the body that it is very difficult to unwind the coils by force and pull its head from its hidden position. This snake also lays small clutches of large eggs, around which it tightly coils to incubate them. Ball pythons feed on small mammals and ground birds.

© Johan Marais

Above

Family: Pythonidae
Common Name: Boelen's python
Scientific Name: *Liasis boeleni*
Location: Highlands of West Irian, Island of New Guinea

This highly arboreal, mountainous jungle-dwelling species is closely related to a number of Pacific Island species whose habits have not been well documented. It is one of the few snake species to live at high altitudes: up to 10,000 feet (3,000 m). It feeds on mammals and birds and, like other pythons, coils around its eggs to incubate them.

Opposite, top

Family: Pythonidae
Common Name: Diamond python
Scientific Name: *Morelia spilotes spilotes*
Location: Australia and New Guinea

This large (up to 13 feet [4 m]) arboreal constrictor is highly variable in coloration and pattern, and interbreeds readily with what is considered a subspecies, the carpet python, *Morelia spilotes variegata*. *Morelia* feeds on birds, mammals, and lizards.

Opposite, bottom

Family: Pythonidae
Common Name: Black-headed python
Scientific Name: *Aspidites melanocephalus*
Location: Northern Australia

The habitat includes wet, coastal forests and nearly arid regions. This is a nocturnal species and feeds on a variety of mammals, birds, and reptiles, including snakes. This is a rare species characterized by its black head and anterior neck. Most adults are not more than 5 feet (1.5 m) in length.

© David T. Roberts

© R. Reed

This page, top

Family: Pythonidae
Common Name: Green tree
python
Scientific Name: *Chondropython viridis*
Location: New Guinea and
northeastern Australia (Cape York)

This is a highly arboreal species
with a prehensile-like tail and enlarged front teeth for capturing
birds. It also feeds readily on mammals and reptiles. Interestingly, the
green tree python looks very similar
to the South American emerald tree
boa. They are the same color with a
slightly different pattern. Young in
both species are brightly colored (in
the boa, they are red, and in the python, some are bright yellow and
others are red) and turn green in
about six or eight months. Both species have adopted the same resting
positions with head drooping downward in the looped body coils. However, unlike the boa, the python lays
eggs, rather than giving birth to live
young. The python descends from
the trees in order to lay its eggs,
around which it coils, like other pythons. Green tree pythons may also
spend considerable time on the
ground hunting for rats.

This page, bottom

Family: Pythonidae
Common Name: Bismarck ringed
python
Scientific Name: *Bothrochilus boa*
Location: Bismarck Archipelago of
Papua New Guinea

A very small, rare species, their
maximum size is 5 to 6 feet (1.5 to
1.8 m). They feed mostly on small
rodents and hunt their prey in moist
forested areas as well as in cultivated
fields and in and around human hab-
itation. This is an extraordinarily at-
tractive species and is highly sought
after by the pet trade.

This page, top

Family: Pythonidae
Common Name: African rock python
Scientific Name: *Python sebae*
Location: Non-desert areas of Africa south of the Sahara to southern Africa

An inhabitant of moist grasslands and savannas, this water-loving species is also at home in drier regions. It is the largest of the African snakes, reaching lengths of up to 20 feet (6 m). A powerful constrictor, the species feeds on small mammals as well as young antelope and pigs. The female lays up to 100 eggs.

This page, bottom

Family: Pythonidae
Common Name: Calabar or burrowing python
Scientific Name: *Calabaria reinhardtii*
Location: West Africa

A burrowing species of moist, tropical rain forests, this cylindrical, stump-tailed constrictor generally does not exceed 3 feet (1 m) in length. Its head and tail are nearly indistinguishable from each other, as the tail is equally blunt and darkly colored and the diminutive, dark eyes are nearly imperceptible. The species feeds on small mammals and coils into a tight ball with its head hidden in the middle of its body folds when disturbed.

Above

Family: Colubridae
Common Name: Smooth green snake
Scientific Name: *Opheodrys vernalis*
Location: Eastern and central United States and northeastern Mexico

   This is one of several innocuous small green snakes that are often seen basking in the tops of low bushes and shrubs in humid areas. It rarely grows to 2 feet (60 cm) in length and is about the width of your little finger. Its diet consists of insects, spiders, and caterpillars, and sometimes includes small amphibians and lizards.

This page, top

Family: Colubridae
Common Name: Chicken snake or yellow rat snake
Scientific Name: *Elaphe obsoleta quadrivittata*
Location: Coastal southeastern United States

This inhabitant of wooded thickets, swamps, old buildings, and similar habitats throughout the coastal plain is a plucky species. When disturbed, it quickly turns to face its molester, raising the front part of its body in a vertical S, and, opening its mouth wide, hisses loudly as it rapidly vibrates its tail.

This page, bottom

Family: Colubridae
Common Name: Long-nosed snake
Scientific Name: *Rhinocheilus lecontei*
Location: South central and southwestern United States and adjacent Mexico

A small species averaging less than 3 feet (1 m) in size, it tends to live in dry prairie and scrubby desert. This little constrictor feeds on lizards and small rodents and derives its name from its slightly upturned, pointed snout, which aids the snake in digging. It is oviparous (egg-laying).

Opposite

Family: Colubridae
Common Name: Long-nosed tree snake
Scientific Name: *Ahaetulla prasinus*
Location: Southeast Asia

This vinelike, rear-fanged, and mildly venomous snake inhabits forests and bushes in moist areas where it feeds on lizards and, occasionally, amphibians. Vine snakes may reach 6 feet (1.8 m) in length and are thin and whiplike. This snake is unique in that it has horizontal pupils and a high degree of binocular vision that enables it to pick out cryptically colored lizards that otherwise would not be visible within the environment. Bites from this snake are rare and often result only in some minor swelling and pain at the bite site.

This page, top

Family: Colubridae
Common Name: Blunt-headed tree snake
Scientific Name: *Imantodes cenchoa*
Location: Central America and northern South America

An arboreal species that finds its home in trees, bushes, and, particularly, moist areas with epiphytic plants. Its diet consists mainly of lizards and frogs. It is highly adapted to its arboreal life-style and can extend its body horizontally to traverse wide expanses between branches. Adults may be as much as 4 feet (1.2 m) in length.

This page, bottom

Family: Colubridae
Common Name: Malaysian rat snake
Scientific Name: *Zaocys fuscus*
Location: Malay Archipelago

This is a large, fast, racerlike snake that is found in a variety of habitats from moist riverbanks to human habitations. It feeds on rodents, frogs, and other snakes. It is frequently used in snake shows and exhibitions. It reaches lengths in excess of 7 feet (2.1 m). It has relatively large eyes, which is a sign of a diurnal animal or one active during daylight hours.

Family: Colubridae
Common Name: Boomslang
Scientific Name: *Dispholidus typus*
Location: Tropical and southern Africa

A highly venomous, rear-fanged, arboreal species. Its bright large eyes perceive the slightest movement of amphibians, lizards, and birds from its perch in shrubs and bushes. Active during the day, it is a common species that varies in color from powder blue to brilliant green. Boomslangs inflate and expand their throats when angry. It is one of the few colubrid species capable of inflicting a bite fatal to humans.

Family: Colubridae
Common Name: Variegated or spotted slug eater
Scientific Name: *Duberria variegata*
Location: Zululand and Mozambique, southern Africa

This is a tiny animal, with a maximum size of 15 inches (39 cm). It lives in sandy forestlands and feeds almost entirely on slugs. Not much is known about this species. It produces about two dozen very small (less than 4 inches [90 mm]) young at a time.

Family: Colubridae
Common Name: Cape file snake
Scientific Name: *Mehelya capensis*
Location: Western and southern Africa

This species grows to about 4 to 6 feet (1.2 to 1.8 m). It gets its name from its extremely coarse scales. It frequents marshes and other wetlands and is often encountered around cultivated fish ponds where it hunts other snakes and amphibians. Nonvenomous, it seizes other snakes with its powerful jaws and constricts them within its coils. It lays about a dozen eggs at a time.

Family: Colubridae
Common Name: Spotted or
rhombic skaapsteker
Scientific Name: *Psammophylax
rhombeatus*
Location: Southern Africa

This snake grows to a maximum length of 3 feet (1 m). It inhabits dry grassland. This is one of a number of species of similar snakes whose diet includes lizards, frogs, small rodents, birds, and other snakes. It is highly terrestrial, quick and agile, and largely diurnal. The female lays eggs in underground shelters and the female guards the eggs.

Family: Colubridae
Common Name: Quill-snouted
snake
Scientific Name: *Xenocalamus
bicolor*
Location: Northern South Africa

This animal lives in desert regions where it burrows with the aid of its highly modified, flattened, and hooked snout. This is a nocturnal species and is believed to feed on small burrowing snakes and burrowing limbless lizards. These small snakes grow to a maximum size of 15 inches (500 mm). They are oviparous.

© John Visser

This page, top

Family: Colubridae
Common Name: Common egg-eater
Scientific Name: *Dasypeltis scabra*
Location: Africa, south of the Sahara

This snake grows to approximately 27 inches (70 cm), and it is found in a variety of habitats throughout its wide range. It feeds entirely on birds' eggs. The egg is ingested by the modified jaws, crushed by vertebral spurs, and the eggshell is regurgitated. This snake lays eggs.

© David T. Roberts

This page, bottom

Family: Colubridae
Common Name: Mud snake
Scientific Name: *Farancia abacura*
Location: Eastern and southern United States

This glossy black-and-red beauty frequents the muddy bottoms and dense aquatic vegetation of swamps, ponds, roadside ditches, and other wetland habitats. The species feeds almost exclusively on the siren, *Amphiuma* species. Lengths range from 3 to 7 feet (1 to 2.1 m).

Family: Colubridae
Common Name: Western hognose snake
Scientific Name: *Heterodon nasicus*
Location: Central United States from southern Canada to northern Mexico

Hognose snakes are found throughout much of the United States and are well known for their general unwillingness to bite and their display when endangered. When threatened, hognose snakes hiss loudly, spread their necks and flatten their heads like a cobra, open their mouths, stick out their tongues, and roll on their backs, feigning death after a drama of contortions. Hognose snakes feed principally on toads and other amphibians. These snakes grow to 15 to 24 inches (36 to 60 cm).

Family: Colubridae
Common Name: Desert hook-nosed snake
Scientific Name: *Gyalopion quadrangularis*
Location: Southern Arizona, United States, south to Mexico

A small (7 to 14 inches [18 to 36 cm]) burrowing species about which little is known. It is a desert dweller. The species is oviparous and feeds on spiders, centipedes, and scorpions. The western form is known to make popping sounds with its cloaca or excretory opening when alarmed. It is distinguished by its short, rather stout body and the hooked scale at the tip of its snout.

© John D. Lutz/Dembinsky Photo Associates

© David T. Roberts

Opposite

Family: Elapidae
Common Name: Brown sea snake
Scientific Name: *Aipysurus laevis*
Location: Coast of northern Australia and New Guinea

This venomous inhabitant of coral reefs gives live birth to about five young. It feeds on fish, which it kills with its highly neurotoxic venom. This is the largest species in the genus and reaches lengths of up to 6 feet (1.8 m). It is dangerous to man only when carelessly handled.

This page, top

Family: Elapidae
Common Name: Spectacled cobra
Scientific Name: *Naja naja naja*
Location: India

This is the snake well known as the snake charmer's cobra. This venomous species reaches lengths of 7.5 feet (2.3 m) and accounts for many snakebites. The only habitat in which it does not occur is dense forests.

This page, below

Family: Elapidae
Common Name: Yellow-lipped sea krait
Scientific Name: *Laticauda colubrina*
Location: Coastal waters of New Guinea and the Pacific Islands, Southeast Asia to Japan

It is sometimes referred to as the Fiji Island sea snake and is one of the few sea snakes that has well-developed ventral scales and leaves the water to lay eggs on land.

© R. Reed

© R. Reed

This page, top

Family: Elapidae
Common Name: Cape cobra
Scientific Name: *Naja nivea*
Location: South Africa

This inhabitant of grasslands and open plains has a particularly toxic venom, which it uses to kill snakes and lizards as well as mammals. Bites from this species are often fatal. Maximum size is 5.5 feet (1.7 m).

This page, bottom

Family: Elapidae
Common Name: Egyptian cobra
Scientific Name: *Naja haje*
Location: Most of Africa and the Arabian Peninsula

Despite its name, this very venomous species is found in nearly all habitats and, in particular, low flatlands throughout most of Africa. It reaches 8 feet (2.5 m) and comes in a variety of patterns and colorations. Some races feign death if pressed by an intruder, while others may be aggressive.

© Johan Marais

© John Visser

This page, top

Family: Elapidae
Common Name: Rinkhals
Scientific Name: *Hemachatus haemachatus*
Location: South Africa and Zimbabwe

This snake inhabits grasslands and relatively dry areas. Its maximum size is about 5 feet (1.5 m). Its food consists of snakes, rodents, and amphibians, including toads. Although its venom is highly toxic, it is more feared for its ability to spit its venom at the eyes of an intruder.

This page, bottom

Family: Elapidae
Common Name: Black mamba
Scientific Name: *Dendroaspis polylepis*
Location: Central to southern Africa

This large (up to 14 feet [4.3 m]), exceptionally dangerous venomous snake inhabits dry forests and brushy hillsides. Its nervous, aggressive nature and large size make it a formidable animal that is highly feared by local people. Its diet consists of birds and small mammals.

This page, top

Family: Elapidae
Common Name: Green mamba
Scientific Name: *Dendroaspis angusticeps*
Location: East Africa

This arboreal counterpart of the black mamba, although just as venomous, is not nearly as feared because it is not as aggressive. It lives in low bushes and trees where it feeds on frogs, lizards, and birds. It grows to be about 8 feet (2.5 m) and is oviparous.

This page, bottom

Family: Elapidae
Common Name: Shield-nose snake
Scientific Name: *Aspidelaps scutatus*
Location: Central South Africa

This is a small, desert-dwelling species rarely reaching 2.5 feet (80 cm). This stout cobralike snake spreads a partial hood when aroused. It feeds on lizards, snakes, and frogs, although it may also eat small mammals and birds. It is oviparous.

© Johan Marais

© Johan Marais

This page, top

Family: Elapidae
Common Name: Loveridge's garter snake
Scientific Name: *Elapsoidea love-ridgei loveridgei*
Location: Kenya and northern Tanzania
This small (16 to 20 inch [40–50 cm]), slender nocturnal snake has a mildly toxic venom, which it uses to kill small snakes, lizards, and amphisbaenians. It inhabits dry woodlands and savannas.

This page, bottom

Family: Elapidae
Common Name: Death adder
Scientific Name: *Acanthophis pyrrhus*
Location: Western and central Australia
   Although short and stout with a large head like a viper, this elapid has a highly neurotoxic venom. The snake generally does not get larger than 2 feet (61 cm) in length. It inhabits dry, sandy, and grassy areas and feeds on lizards, mammals, and small birds. Rather than pursuing its prey, it lies in wait and may use its brightly colored tail as a lure.

This page, top

Family: Viperidae
Subfamily: Viperinae
Common Name: Long-nosed viper
Scientific Name: *Vipera ammodytes*
Location: Eastern Europe

This inhabitant of dry, rocky hillsides has a sharply upturned snout. It feeds on small mammals and birds, although it may also eat lizards. It is sometimes called a sand viper. It is ovoviviparous. It reaches about 2 feet (61 cm) in length.

This page, bottom

Family: Viperidae
Subfamily: Viperinae
Common Name: Russell's viper
Scientific Name: *Daboia russelli*
Location: Southern Asia

This large viper attains lengths of up to 6 feet (1.8 m). It is considered extremely dangerous and accounts for a great many bites and human fatalities. Active at night. It gives live birth to as many as 70 young at a time, which makes it a very prolific and common species.

© Johan Marais

© Ron Whitaker

Family: Viperidae
Subfamily: Viperinae
Common Name: Saw-scaled viper
Scientific Name: *Echis carinatus*
Location: East Africa, Middle East through Southeast Asia

This small (up to 2 feet [61 cm]), highly irritable viper has a highly toxic venom that produces massive hemorrhaging. It is found in sandy, rocky, open areas but may also occur in a variety of other habitats.

Family: Viperidae
Subfamily: Viperinae
Common Name: Puff adder
Scientific Name: *Bitis arietans*
Location: Africa south of the Sahara, and Arabian Peninsula

This large, heavy-bodied viper attains lengths of up to 6 feet (1.8 m). It produces large amounts of highly toxic tissue-destroying venom. It inhabits many habitats with the exceptions of deserts and rain forests.

© Rom Whitaker

© Johan Marais

© David T. Roberts

© R. Reed

This page, top

Family: Viperidae
Subfamily: Viperinae
Common Name: Fea's viper
Scientific Name: *Azemiops feae*
Location: Myanmar, Tibet, China, and Vietnam

Very little is known about this species, which generally does not reach 3 feet (1 m) in length. It is presumed to feed on mice and have a toxic venom. It inhabits mountains at the higher elevations.

This page, bottom

Family: Viperidae
Subfamily: Viperinae
Common Name: McMahon's viper
Scientific Name: *Eristicophis macmahoni*
Location: Afghanistan and Pakistan

This desert-dwelling species rarely exceeds 2 feet (61 cm) in length. It feeds on small mammals and lizards and is a burrowing species.

This page, top

Family: Viperidae
Subfamily: Crotalinae
Common Name: Tropical rattlesnake or Mexican cascavel
Scientific Name: *Crotalus durissus culminatus*
Location: Mexico

This is a highly dangerous snake with an extremely toxic venom that has a strong neurotoxic component. It occurs in dry plateaus and is common on farms and ranches where it is greatly feared. It reaches lengths of up to 6 feet (1.8 m). It gives birth to up to two dozen live young. When surprised, this snake assumes an elevated coiled posture with head drawn back, ready to strike.

© R. Reed

This page, bottom

Family: Viperidae
Subfamily: Crotalinae
Common Name: Cottonmouth or water moccasin
Scientific Name: *Agkistrodon piscivorus*
Location: Southeastern United States

This denizen of wetlands receives its name from its characteristic threat position, with its mouth open wide, exposing the white cotton-colored interior. It is venomous and can cause a fatal bite if not treated promptly. As many as 15 live young are born in late summer or early autumn.

© John D. Lutz/Dembinsky Photo Associates

Opposite

Family: Viperidae
Subfamily: Crotalinae
Common Name: Urutu
Scientific Name: *Bothrops alternatus*
Location: Central South America

This beautiful, large, and potentially dangerous pit viper reaches lengths of up to 5 feet (1.5 m). It gives birth to live young. It frequents moist forests, streams, streambanks, ponds, and small lakes where it feeds on small mammals and frogs. This is a relatively peaceful snake, and it has a moderately toxic venom.

appendix one:

ZOOS WITH SIGNIFICANT SNAKE COLLECTIONS

AUSTRALIA

Adelaide Zoological Gardens
Adelaide, South Australia

Taronga Zoo
P.O. Box 20
Mosman, New South Wales

Royal Melbourne Zoological Gardens
P.O. Box 74
Parkville, Victoria 3052

Perth Zoo
P.O. Box 489
South Perth 6151

BELGIUM

Royal Society of Antwerp
Koningen Astridplein 26
B-2000 Antwerpen

BRAZIL

Rio Zoo
Rio de Janiero 20940

CANADA

Calgary Zoological Society
P.O. Box 3036 Station B
Calgary, Alberta T2M 4R8

Reptile Breeding Foundation
P.O. Box 1450
Picton, Ontario K0K 2T0

Metropolitan Toronto Zoo
P.O. Box 280
West Hill, Ontario M1E 4R5

Société Zoologique de Granby, Inc.
37 Rue Bourget
Granby, Québec J2G 1E8

Aquarium du Québec
1675m avenue du Parc
Sainte-Foy, Québec G1W 4S3

CZECHOSLOVAKIA

Zoologicka Zahrada Jihlava
58601 Jihlava

GERMANY

Lobbecke Museum and Aquazoo
Postfach 11 20
Kaiserswerther Strasse 380
Dusseldorf 1

HUNGARY

Mecseki Kulturpark
Domorkapu
7627 Pecs.

INDIA

Poona Serpentarium
Katraj
Poona Satara Rd.
Pune 411 046

IRELAND

Dublin Zoo
Phoenix Park
Dublin 8

JAPAN

Sendai Yagiyama Zoological Park
43 Tagiyama-honcho
1-Chome
Sendai

POLAND

Weilkopolski Park Zoologiczny
61-083 Poznan
ul. Bowarna 25

REPUBLIC OF SOUTH AFRICA

East London Aquarium
Queens Park
East London

Manyeleti Reptile Centre
P.O. Manyeleti 1362

Johannesburg Zoological Gardens
Jan Smuts Ave.
Parkview 2193

Transvaal Snake Park Ltd.
P.O. Box 97
Halfway House
1685 Transvaal

SINGAPORE

Singapore Zoological Gardens
80 Mandai Lake Rd.
Singapore 2572

SWITZERLAND

Tierpark Dahlholzli
Dalmaziquai 149
Bern CH-3005

Zoo Zurich
CH 0844 Zurich

U.S.S.R.

Alma-Atinskii Zoopark
Esenberlin-Str. 166
Zoological Gardens in Alma-Ata
480007 Alma-Ata

Moscow Zoo
123820 Moscow
B. Gruzinskaya 1

UNITED KINGDOM

Blackpool Zoo
East Park Drive
Blackpool, Lancastershire

Linton Zoological Gardens
Hadstock Rd.
Linton, Cambridgeshire

Liverpool Museum
Liverpool

Zoological Society of London
Regent's Park
London

Cannon Aquarium and Vivarium
Manchester Museum
University of Manchester
Manchester 13

Glasgow Zoological Gardens
Calderpark
Uddingston, Glasgow
Scotland G71 7RZ

UNITED STATES

Arizona Sonora Desert Museum
2021 N. Kinney Rd.
Tucson, AZ 85743

Los Angeles Zoo
5333 Zoo Drive
Los Angeles, CA 90027

San Diego Zoo
P.O. Box 551
San Diego, CA 92112

Denver Zoological Gardens
City Park
Denver, CO 80205

National Zoological Park
3000 Connecticut Ave., NW
Washington, D.C. 20008

Central Florida Zoo
Box 309
Lake Monroe, FL 32747

Metro Zoo
12400 Southwest 152nd St.
Miami, FL 33177

Zoo Atlanta
800 Cherokee Ave., SE
Atlanta, GA 30315

Chicago Zoological Park
300 Golf Rd.
Brookfield, IL 60513

Lincoln Park Zoo
2200 North Cannon Dr.
Chicago, IL 60614

Louisville Zoological Gardens
1100 Trevilian Way
P.O. Box 37250
Louisville, KY 40233

Baltimore Zoo
Druid Hill Park
Baltimore, MD 21217

Detroit Zoological Park
8450 West Ten Mile Rd.
P.O. Box 39
Royal Oak, MI 48068-0039

Minnesota Zoological Garden
12101 Johnny Cake Rd.
Apple Valley, MN 55124

St. Louis Zoo
Forest Park
St. Louis, MO 63110

New York Zoological Park
185th St. and Southern Blvd.
Bronx, NY 10460

Buffalo Zoological Gardens
Delaware Park
Buffalo, NY 14214

Burnet Park Zoo
P.O. Box 146
Liverpool, NY 13088

Central Park Zoo
830 Fifth Ave.
New York, NY 10021

Staten Island Zoological Society
614 Broadway
Staten Island, NY 10310

Cincinnati Zoo and Botanical Garden
3400 Vine St.
Cincinnati, OH 45220

Cleveland Metroparks Zoo
3900 Brookside Park Dr.
Cleveland, OH 44109

Columbus Zoological Park
9990 Riverside Dr.
Box 400
Howell, OH 43065

Toledo Zoological Society
2700 Broadway
Toledo, OH 43609

Riverbanks Zoological Park
500 Wildlife Parkway
Columbia, SC 29210

Knoxville Zoological Park
Box 6040
Knoxville, TN 37914

Memphis Zoological Gardens and
Aquarium
200 Galloway Ave.
Memphis, TN 38112-9990

Gladys Porter Zoo
500 Ringgold St.
Brownsville, TX 78520

Dallas Zoo
621 East Clarendon Dr.
Dallas, TX 75203-2969

Fort Worth Zoological Park
2727 Zoological Park Dr.
Fort Worth, TX 76110

San Antonio Zoological Society
3930 North St. Mary's St.
San Antonio, TX 78212

Woodland Park Zoological Gardens
5500 Phinney Ave. N.
Seattle, WA 98103

Milwaukee County Zoo
10001 West Bluemound Rd.
Milwaukee, WI 53226

appendix two:

SNAKES IN THE WILD

It is extremely difficult to walk into a wild area and see snakes. Some wildlife refuges have walkways that lead the public through areas in which snakes are known to abound. Even then, it takes a keen eye and optimal weather conditions to see snakes. Most of the time, the best you can hope for is to see a snake crossing a road or basking in the sun. Driving slowly through regions where snakes occur in large numbers during the early part of the night or after a warm rain is often the best way to see snakes crossing the road. Remember, look and photograph, but *do not touch and capture*. Be aware that the snake may be venomous or, even if not venomous, may give you a nasty bite. Attempting to capture or collect snakes may be a violation of local or national law. In most cases, zoological parks do not keep large collections of endemic species because limited space is allocated for endangered species programs, so you may not be able to donate the snake you capture to a local zoo.

Most herpetology departments of local zoos or natural history museums or zoology departments of local universities can give you information on local refuges and parks where snakes may be seen.

Local and national herpetological societies are also sources of information on snakes. The following is a list of organizations to contact:

American Society of Ichthyologists and Herpetologists
Department of Zoology
Southern Illinois University
Carbondale, IL 62901-6501

Herpetologists' League, Inc.
Texas Parks and Wildlife Dept.
4200 Smith School Road
Austin, TX 78744

Society for the Study of Amphibians and Reptiles
% Dr. Douglas H. Taylor
Department of Zoology
Miami University
Oxford, OH 45056

British Herpetological Society
% Zoological Society of London
Regents Park
London NW1
United Kingdom

Australian Herpetologists' League
GPO 864
Sydney 2001
N.S.W.
Australia

Canadian Herpetological Society
P.O. Box 130
Station G
Toronto M4M 4E8
Canada

A list of local herpetological societies is available on-line from:

Herpetological On-Line Network
P.O. Box 52261
Philadelphia, PA 19115
Modem access: 215-464-3562

appendix three:

RECOMMENDED BOOKS

This is a short list of recommended books. There are many more that you are likely to find at a good university library.

Behler, John, and F. Wayne King. *The Audubon Society Field Guide to North American Reptiles and Amphibians.* New York: Alfred A. Knopf, 1979.

Branch, Bill. *Bill Branch's Field Guide to the Snakes and Other Reptiles of Southern Africa.* Sanibel Island, FL: Ralph Curtis Books, 1988.

Coborn, John. *Snakes and Lizards: Their Care and Breeding in Captivity.* Sanibel Island, FL: Ralph Curtis Books, 1987.

Cogger, Harold G. *Reptiles and Amphibians of Australia.* Sydney: A. H. & A. W. Reed.

Conant, Roger. *A Field Guide to Reptiles and Amphibians of Eastern and Central North America.* (The Peterson Field Guide Series.) 2nd ed. Boston: Houghton Mifflin Co., 1975.

Crompton, John. *The Snake.* New York: Nick Lyons Books, 1987.

Daniel, J. C. *The Book of Indian Reptiles.* Bombay: Bombay Natural History Society, 1983.

Ditmars, Raymond L. *Reptiles of the World: Tortoises and Turtles, Crocodilians, Lizards and Snakes of the Eastern and Western Hemispheres.* New York: The Macmillan Co., 1927. (Note: A classic.)

Ditmars, Raymond L. *Strange Animals I Have Known.* New York: Brewer, Warren & Putnam Inc., 1931. (Note: Another classic.)

Freiberg, Marcos. *Snakes of South America.* Neptune, NJ: T.F.H. Publications Inc., Ltd., 1982.

Halliday, Tim R., and Kraig Adler, eds. *The Encyclopedia of Reptiles and Amphibians.* New York: Facts on File Inc., 1986.

Kauffeld, Carl. *Snakes and Snake Hunting.* Garden City, NY: Hanover House, 1957. (Note: A classic.)

Klauber, Laurence M. *Rattlesnakes: Their Habits, Life Histories, and Influence on Mankind.* Abridged Edition. Berkeley: University of California Press, 1982.

Kuntz, Robert E. *Snakes of Taiwan.* Taipei, Taiwan: U.S. Naval Medical Research Unit No. 2, 1963.

Lancini V., Abdem R. *Serpientes de Venezuela.* Ernesto Armitano, ed. Caracas, Venezuela, 1979.

Marais, Johan. *Snake Versus Man: A Guide to Dangerous and Common Harmless Snakes of Southern Africa.* Johannesburg: Macmillan South Africa Pty Ltd., 1985.

Mehrtens, John M. *Living Snakes of the World in Color.* New York: Sterling Publishing Co., Inc., 1987.

Minton, Sherman A., Jr., Herndon G. Dowling, and Findlay E. Russell. *Poisonous Snakes of the World: A Manual For Use By U.S. Amphibious Forces.* Dept. of the Navy. U.S. Gov't. Printing Office, Washington, D.C. Publication # NAVMED P-5099 (1965).

Obst, Fritz Jürgen, Klaus Richter, and Udo Jacob. *The Completely Illustrated Atlas of Reptiles and Amphibians for the Terrarium.* Neptune City, NJ: T.F.H. Publications, Inc., 1988.

Parker, H. W., and A. G. C. Grandison. *Snakes—A Natural History.* Ithaca, NY: British Museum (Natural History)/Cornell University Press, 1977.

Seigel, Richard A., Joseph T. Collins, and Susan S. Novak, eds. *Snakes: Ecology and Evolutionary Biology.* New York: Macmillan Publishing Co., 1987.

Shaw, Charles E., and Sheldon Campbell. *Snakes of the American West.* New York: Alfred A. Knopf, 1974.

Smith, Hobart M. *Snakes As Pets.* 4th ed. Neptune City, NJ: T.F.H. Publications, Inc., 1977.

Stanek, V. J. *Introducing Poisonous Snakes.* London: Spring Books, 1960.

Wilson, Larry David, and John R. Meyer. *The Snakes of Honduras.* Milwaukee, WI: Milwaukee Public Museum, 1982.